HENRY FOOL

HENRY FOOL
Hal Hartley

faber and faber

First published in 1998
by Faber and Faber Limited
3 Queen Square London WC1N 3AU

Photoset by Parker Typesetting Service, Leicester
Printed in England by Clays Ltd, St Ives plc

A CIP record for this book
is available from the British Library
ISBN 0–571–19519–9

2 4 6 8 10 9 7 5 3 1

CONTENTS

RESPONDING TO NATURE
Hal Hartley in conversation with Graham Fuller

Writing the introduction to the *Amateur* screenplay book in 1994, I
observed that that particular Hal Hartley film was 'both a
continuation and a departure' from his three previous features. It
was a continuation in that, aesthetically and philosophically, it was
'of a piece' with *The Unbelievable Truth* (1989), *Trust* (1990), and
Simple Men (1992). It was a departure in that those earlier films
were romantic melodramas, whereas *Amateur* was a romantic
thriller with a tragic arc and a whiff of Expressionism. It wasn't a
radical departure, however, for the evolutionary developments in
Hartley's work are extremely subtle. Ultimately, too, categorizing
his films according to genre may be unhelpful. Melodramas?
Thrillers? If so, they are unlike those made by anyone else. Try
comparing *Trust* to *All That Heaven Allows*, say, or *Amateur* to *The
Getaway*, and one comes unstuck. What Hartley does is take
generic structures and pour his cinema into them, turning them
into something that's not altogether unrecognizable but is
uniquely his. What he does is make Hal Hartley films; it sounds
obvious, but it's an irreducible truth.

   Where does *Henry Fool* fit into this? Again it's a continuation
and a departure. We know we're in Hartley country immediately
from the staccato juxtaposition of action-driven scenes and from
the compositional and tonal quality of those scenes: we just know,
all right? But the story itself is driven by the dynamic between two
men – mentor and initiate – instead of by the romantic tension
between a man and a woman, and that's new. Which genre shall
we nervously label this oddity? Although set in Woodside, in the
New York borough of Queens, the film's stranger-in-town-
righting-wrongs set-up suggests a Western. Henry's arrival – he's
seen in longshot, marching toward us from beyond the point
where the sky touches the road – is reminiscent of the beginning of
both *Shane* and *The Searchers*; indeed, Henry is closely related to
the latter's Ethan Edwards: each has a criminal past, is sexually or
romantically drawn to a doomed older woman, has a troubled
relationship with his protegé, seeks violent revenge on the rape of a

female child, and ultimately has no place in society (although in Hartley's film that issue is complicated by the ambiguous ending).

That for the first time there are as many as fourteen major characters and a six-year time frame, that the title has a Shakespearean resonance, hint at *Henry Fool*'s aspiring to saga or epic tragedy status, the unseen correlatives of which are Simon's scabrous epic poem and Henry's book-length confession. Hartley pulls this epic-ness off, too, albeit inside a more minimalist canvas than usual. Life rolls on inexorably in *Henry Fool*. People change – two of them die. A garbage disposal man with no voice or apparent future becomes a Nobel Prize-winning author. A nymphomaniac becomes a housewife; she bears a child and it grows. Even the physical terrain changes: the espresso bar gives way to a nightclub. But Hartley's concern, of course, is more with the epic nature of change in his characters' interior lives than how their physical selves or their environment may change. He says in the following interview that his *modus operandi* for shooting the film was simply, given his limited budget, to 'respond to nature . . . to sculpt, to make an artifice, to strive to construct a powerful, correct image out of what exists there'. It's an idea that applies to the texture of the drab Woodside street down which Henry takes Pearl home on his bike and the iridescently glowing basement apartment where they have their fateful encounter years later, but most powerfully to the intangible psychological and behavioural shifts that he has prescribed for his characters in his script and that have found their existence in the actors' performances. In other words, it is in responding to the roller-coaster momentum of human nature and photographing it in his familiarly terse, flab-free style that *Henry Fool* achieves its emotional girth, its tragic sway.

The conversation with Hartley printed here took place in his roomy but spartan office between Chelsea and Greenwich Village in Manhattan on 14 March 1998. Walter Donohue of Faber had originally given me the opportunity to interview Hartley for the screenplay book of *Simple Men* and *Trust* and subsequently for the *Amateur* book, and this was our fifth interview in all. Since it's always a joy and an education to talk to the affably passionate Hal, I hope this is one of those epics that goes on and on.

Graham Fuller
April 1998

GRAHAM FULLER: Henry Fool *is a return to a full-length narrative after your experiment in form with* Flirt. *What prompted that experimentation in the first place?*

HAL HARTLEY: The impulse to make *Flirt* essentially came out of my boredom with telling feature-length stories. I think it's legitimate to get bored sometimes with the thing you are supposed to be good at, and then make exercises or experiments for yourself through which you can study your inclinations and look at the tools you use from a different angle to keep them vital. Doing creative work, the thing that one tries to avoid is becoming habitual, and when I embarked on *Flirt* it just felt like the right time for me to indulge myself in an exercise, even though none of the three stories in *Flirt* is particularly experimental in terms of narrative. But limiting my palette so extremely and just saying, 'I'm going to film the same script three times and try my damnedest to discover new modes of rendering the story and the ideas,' was interesting. Actually, I do that a lot in terms of the smaller video pieces I make and a lot of the writing I do that never becomes a film.

GF: *What were the 'habitual' elements of the full-length feature format that you wanted to step away from?*

HH: The basic feature film has a lot of built-in expectations. People want that particular rhythmic plot and character development and conclusion. That's great – I love that. But, after *Amateur*, I just felt that I'd done about as much of that as I wanted to for the moment. I wanted to discover other things. Some of them were quite mundane.

GF: *How do you mean?*

HH: For example, I don't like establishing shots for their own sake, so I've always tried to make the shot that establishes an environment become something else. If you broke all of the pictures I've made down to each individual shot, I think one thing you'd see most of the time is a striving to make real poetic, grammatical use of the image that I start with. However, I'd never been satisfied with my work in terms of the way I rendered environment and space. On *Flirt*, I went to foreign places to kind of shock myself into an awareness of different environments and ways of seeing them. I think I got halfway there and began to see ways of moving forward when we were working on the second part in Berlin. By the time I'd finished that part, I said to myself, 'I now have to try to make a silent movie.' The point was that I would be forced to turn anything that was related in language into an activity, which really opened up the rules of the game. I actually stayed within the rules, but it meant there was no reason why I couldn't add new scenes, because before I was just trying to render something that was spoken. So that was a real key and when I got to Tokyo for the third part, I was fascinated by the space and I dedicated myself to looking and showing, rather than relating, through the image. It forced me into being aware of environments. I feel the Japanese section of *Flirt* is the best work I've done, and I knew it while I was shooting it. I said to myself, 'I'm really getting somewhere now. I'm really beginning to improve in this area that I've always been dissatisfied with. And when I go back home, I've got to look at my world as a foreign place' – although I was already becoming anxious to work in English again. The whole exercise did what an exercise is supposed to do. It made movie-making mysterious to me again. So I came back and found Woodside, Queens, in New York City, which is where we shot *Henry Fool*, and I kept looking at it like it is: a different planet.

GF: Henry Fool *is your first feature that isn't driven by a relationship between a man and a woman, but between two male characters – Simon and Henry, who becomes Simon's mentor. What prompted the shift away from the romantic framework?*
HH: First of all, I wanted to make a larger story. All of my films have stayed very close to a particular relationship between two people and they've been compact in terms of time. It's something that I am naturally drawn to, and it has something to do with this poetic economy of images and dialogue that I like, because I think it's something that movies do well. With *Henry Fool*, I wanted to make a story that addressed a lot of different issues. I was still interested in having a relationship between a man and a woman – Henry and Fay – but this time I didn't want it to be the middle of the movie. So, yes, the spine of *Henry Fool* is the relationship between Henry and Simon and the tragedy of their misunderstanding.

x

GF: *The crisis comes when Simon doesn't stand by his agreement to withdraw his poem from the publisher when he refuses to publish Henry's book.*

HH: Yes. Neither one of them, I think, is wrong. It's just the way things are. It felt like a very traditional story to me. I was thinking of a lot of big, literary works, like *Don Quixote* and *Faust*. I drew on a lot of classic models of epic films, including *Dr Zhivago* and *Lawrence of Arabia*, with the intention of creating a story like that in my own medium and my own mode.

GF: *'Hal', of course, is a diminutive of Henry. Is your name Henry?*

HH: No, my name is Harold. But, yes, Hal is short for Henry.

GF: *It made me speculate about your own identification with Henry in the film. Hal is also one of the names Falstaff has for the young Prince Henry in* Henry IV, Part I *and Part II, and, of course, the boy king turns his back on his old friend just as Simon turns his back on Henry. Even though Henry is the betrayed, not the betrayer in* Henry Fool, *it would appear to be a direct allusion.* Henry Fool *is definitely Falstaffian in appearance and behavior.*

HH: I was reaching for archetypes and traditional examples everywhere. I consciously drew on the Falstaff–Prince Hal relationship, although it's something I know only second-hand; I didn't go back and reread Shakespeare's plays. Henry is also partially inspired by Mephistopheles in *Faust*, which I've looked at a lot in the past four or five years. And I drew on the Kaspar Hauser story – which is something I refer to all the time in my writing – when I was thinking about Simon, and got real meaning out of it. I'm not quite sure in practical terms what it is you get when you take from other stories and myths, but I know I've gotten a lot of sustenance from them.

GF: *A word that keeps cropping up in your script is 'vocation'.*

HH: Yes. It's certainly a part of Henry's vocabulary. What he tries to teach Simon is that a vocation is a responsibility to an innate talent that you have, and that it's bigger than you. It requires humility, and it's not something you can abuse for financial gain or popularity. That's the kind of mindset Henry represents.

Henry and Simon are parts of anybody who is creative. I certainly recognize the two of them: the one who pontificates and the one who gets on with it. Those two warring factions exist in my own head. It's important to realize that, to be a creative person, you don't necessarily have to be the alpha and omega of knowledge. What makes someone's creativity interesting is that they throw themselves out there for public view without knowing what they're doing. I tried to be very systematic – even academic – about showing that Simon represents certain aspects of creative talent and knowledge while Henry represents others. I didn't, however, want us to be able to see either Henry's confession or Simon's poem, because I didn't want us to get involved with judging them. That wasn't really the issue. It could be that Henry's confession is a great piece of writing even though Simon and the publisher guy dismiss it. I was much more interested in showing how the value of creative activity is often measured by the particular kind of reaction it elicits. I wanted to address that for myself as a creative person who is a commercial item as well. Sometimes I read perfectly nice articles about my work that I can't appreciate. It's a tense argument that people in your business and my business have: Is criticism advertising? Is advertising criticism? If it is, what's the work itself? Is it advertising as well? Is it criticism? These are complex and vital arguments that we have to keep having. I remember the first real problem I had with this was getting good reviews and having to keep myself from getting tangled up in an appreciation of that review. It's that 'I can't buy into the hype' issue.

GF: *Have your films been given positive reviews, which, in your opinion, completely missed the point of what you were trying to say?*
HH: I haven't read reviews of mine in a long time because of this relationship between criticism and advertising. It's very confusing. But, yes, I've had at least one favorable review by a pretty important critic in which I thought she was advertising her own ideas about art she admired and that she wanted to exist in the world. It completely missed the point of the film. Nevertheless, it was a review that was often quoted and helped to sell the film. Really, we have to laugh at ourselves in this predicament. You can't just say, 'Criticism is pointless,' because that would be no different to saying creative activity is pointless. It all stays alive because people argue about it.

I have to add that I have had reviews for my films that were not only good but made valid criticisms that have stuck in my head because they were about something I knew had to be addressed. Again, it comes down to humility. You have to not get an attitude and wall yourself off from criticism. If you feel insecure about something, you should look at it.

GF: *Where did Henry and Simon spring from as characters?*
HH: I've had the idea for the name 'Henry Fool' since I was in college. Back then Henry was a kind of ne'er-do-well. Even in the infancy of my creative development as a writer and a storyteller, there was this inclination to tell a big story about the education and adventures of a particular person. Most of my films have had that kind of *bildungsroman* quality. Anyway, Henry was there at the beginning – I just never knew what to do with him.

Since I made *Trust*, I've been out there as a creative worker advertising myself by being on the road, having my picture taken, and stuff like that, and the whole world has opened up to me. I'd never traveled before becoming a film-maker and so this whole experience has been epic to the extent that it sometimes makes it hard to discuss with people back home what the reality of your life is like. These events and thoughts helped me to shape the idea of the character of Simon, four or five years ago. Initially, I thought he would be an engineer and that he would go though some sort of romance, a lost love thing. So the film started to take shape as a story of a young man's achievement, regret, and self-discovery – which is what I consider most of the really big, great novels are about.

And then I had a personal experience which galvanized everything. I championed somebody's work, which I didn't think was ready to be championed. I did it out of friendship, but it was misguided. I lost the friendship, and it hurt. Suddenly all of these musings that I'd had for five or six years found a concrete, active event that I could shape the whole story around.

I actually don't think the movie has one particular point to it, but I would say that the heart of the story – even though it comes a long way into it and just before the final, seven-years-later passage – is the conversation in the hospital hallway between Henry and Simon. I think everything they say to each other at that point is stuff that

I've said to myself and stuff that I've had to grapple with. It's that whole issue of what Henry's getting at when he accuses Simon: 'You're being popular. Oh my God, that's horrible.' But is it?

GF: *Simon's integrity is also at stake, isn't it?*

HH: Yes, although I don't think Simon sacrifices his integrity when he refuses to stop his book being published. I think at that moment he and Henry both hold on to their integrity. But Simon shouldn't have promised to withdraw his book – that's the moral, I think. You can't put yourself out on a limb for something you don't know about and Simon hadn't read Henry's confession when he made his promise.

If Simon had withdrawn his book he would have been throwing away everything he'd learned from Henry, who taught him the value of his talent and kept reminding him that he'd got to make sacrifices for it, he'd got to go all the way with it, because it's bigger than him and his petty little life. He taught him that the work is everything and that he'd got to get it out there.

GF: *You spoke earlier of the tragedy of their misunderstanding. Can you pinpoint what that is for you?*

HH: It's that Simon broke his promise to his friend. It was a dumb promise, but a promise nevertheless. Everybody's got great intentions, but they crash.

GF: *To what extent do you see Henry as a visitor, in the sense of angel or devil?*

HH: That's the great dichotomy I wanted. Is he the Devil or is he an angel? There's the idea that the Devil was once an angel, too, but he's on the outs with the front office. I've always believed that the Devil has a place in our Western Judeo-Christian sense of morality. Andrew Delbanco has written in *The Death of Satan* how one of the problems of Western society now is that we've lost our appreciation of what the Devil is: he's not scary anymore. Yet I think the Devil of Christian mythology serves a real purpose. As the unseen haphazard cause of things, he symbolizes anarchy and he brings the blood into our interactions with each other; I tried to make Henry represent that without imposing judgment on him. Simon, for example, is deeply affected by Henry's resolve and acquires his own resolve by imitating Henry. Warren, in turn, is influenced by Simon. So it's a domino effect. It's not always for the good. For Amy, who's mean to Simon at the beginning, it's probably good since she starts to become less mean to him; for Warren, it looks good for a while, and then it goes completely wrong. I think Fay benefits; Mom doesn't.

The idea of influence was very important in helping this story come together. I get asked a lot who were my biggest influences. It's always an embarrassing question to answer because I often feel like I'm answering for someone else and I don't want to have that responsibility. I also think we're often influenced by things that we don't even like. In *The Anxiety of Influence*, which is a book of literary criticism that goes over my head, Harold Bloom isolates genius in literary achievements through the ages by examining how different writers have tried to avoid recognition of their influences. He contends that some people have done their best when they've tried to veer away from imitating Shakespeare, say, but have wound up having an excellent dialogue with Shakespeare.

I think that's a pretty useful description of what happens a lot. Certainly I recognize it in my work. For example, I greatly admire Godard, but I don't feel my work is at all like his. I make fiction primarily, but I don't feel he does. I try to do things my own way, but I find I'm having a kind of dialogue with Godard by trying to describe what's beautiful in his work. Of course, even if I try to imitate it, I get it wrong, because I fall into my own groove. I think this is all to the good because I've ended up doing some of my best work this way. It's also kind of embarrassing, but a lot about being creative and being an entertainer is about your relationship to that embarrassment. Even when I talked to Godard once, he said, 'If you see something that's really good, don't be an idiot – just take it and use it. If someone says, "Oh, he stole that from somebody," so what?' You don't have to worry about being super-original, because originality will take care of itself. There's not really anything you can do about it anyway. You can't get up in the morning and sit at the desk and say, 'OK, today I'm going to write something perfectly original, and everybody is going to see how original I am.' When I was a kid, I used to think it worked that way, but in reality it doesn't.

GF: *Godard had his own influences.*

HH: Yes. He got a lot of stuff from Sam Fuller. But a modernist intellectual French-Swiss film-maker trying to copy something from Sam Fuller is bound to turn it into something else – and that something else is what made Godard so interesting.

GF: *Going back to* Henry Fool, *did you write a back story for Simon's family explaining the absence of the father, which is almost a 'structuring absence'?*

HH: I tried to deal with that as much as I could in an early draft, but it got really unwieldy. For me, it was important that Simon did not have a father, so that this seemingly older man could come in, which, of course, is what led to him having sex with Simon's mom and his sister.

In regard to Simon's parents – I think the father probably died in the Vietnam War. I thought a lot about how different Mom could have been and I worked it out that she had once shown some promise as a pianist. I wanted her to be creative because I thought it was very important to get her and Simon into that scene when she's playing the piano, and he says, 'That's nice,' and she makes the distinction between 'nice' and 'unremarkable,' which is a harsh reality. I imagine she got knocked up in high school while she was waiting to get into music school, and then her boyfriend was drafted and got killed so she got stuck with these kids – something mundanely tragic like that.

GF: *Why is Simon disgusted by sex?*

HH: To me, it's more that he's divorced from the sensual world somehow. I didn't want him to react at the beginning of the film when he is watching Warren and Amy have sex. I said to James [Urbaniak, who plays Simon], 'Just watch with fascination like you're watching two pigeons fuck or ants building a mountain.' He drinks it in. Simon definitely senses there's a wall between his reality and experience. I think of Simon as someone who's clear-eyed, but the reason he can't speak is because he sees the world around him clearer than anybody else and it's struck him dumb. I don't think Henry gives him insight, but Henry senses immediately that getting experience of the world must be part and parcel of Simon's education so he can say what's on his mind. I think Henry gives him the eloquence.

GF: *Simon's silence explains his affinity with the Vietnamese woman who works in the World of Donuts shop.*

HH: Yes. She doesn't speak, but she sings when she finds and reads Simon's book. She's the first one to experience Simon's poem. I think whatever it is that Simon has written is an unbelievably clear-eyed view of the world he lives in and that it's completely unmediated by regard for others' propriety. So, of course, it explodes and goes off in many different directions. Some people find it beautiful, other people find it horrendous and pornographic. Certain characters imply that the problem is not so much that it's pornographic, but that it's hurtful.

GF: *Why did you make Fay promiscuous?*

HH: It's just boredom. In contrast with Simon being struck dumb by what he sees around him, it worked well for Fay to be this throbbing sexual being. She also has to spend all that time in the house with her mother, who is a total life-negating person. I feel that Fay must be gasping for air until five-thirty every day when Simon comes home from work and takes over. Simon deals with Mom through the evening, and it's not surprising that Fay's going to go out and get laid.

I have a deep affection for Fay – I just loved the character the moment she came into my head. She was a clear image I didn't think about too much. Right at the beginning, when I started writing, I just knew. There comes that point when you're working on a script when you know that you can sit down and write the whole thing from beginning to end – though, of course, it's only going to be the first draft. At that first sitdown with *Henry Fool*, I knew that, in the first ten pages, I needed to paint broadly an image of a world that's abrasive, desperate, and mundane, and place these characters in the middle of it.

GF: *Did you write Fay with Parker Posey in mind?*

HH: Yes. I had wanted to give her a bigger role for some time and I remember telling her about Fay three years before we did the movie. Tom [Thomas Jay Ryan, who plays Henry] and James [Urbaniak] also got on board very early and all the characters benefited from conversations I had with the actors.

GF: *When Simon gives up working in garbage disposal, Fay types up a resumé and goes for job interviews offscreen. After being initially reluctant to do that, she suddenly seems enthusiastic about it. I sense it's an opportunity for her to grow, but then she conceives the baby and becomes a housewife. We see her carrying the washing, looking bedraggled, and slapping Henry for taking their son to a bar. I felt sad for her, as if life had passed her by.*

HH: I don't know if I agree. I feel that her relationship with her son and even with Henry at the end is fine. She's a good mother who is concerned about the right things. She's still Fay. I didn't want her to go out and become a working girl who suddenly takes charge of her own life. In a way, I think she's in charge of it all the way through. I think the crucial point for her is when she throws the boiling water at Simon and scalds him. She becomes much more sensitive after that, and more focused on being active somehow. She finds her sense of mission raising the kid, making sure Henry doesn't turn him into a little criminal, and making sure Henry goes to work.

So I see a future for Fay, although I don't know if it's a future for her *and* Henry. I could give a lot of false impressions of what's happening there, too, because I've spent so much time with these characters. I tend to think of this story in terms of it having many sequels, as if it were *Star Wars* or something. At the very beginning, I was thinking of *Henry Fool* being part of an epic series of movies about Henry. So when Fay lets Henry go off to Sweden at the end of the film, it opens up all sorts of possibilities.

GF: *Were you conscious of returning to the structural device you used in* The Unbelievable Truth *where a stranger – an ex-con – comes to town and effectively liberates the people there.*

HH: Yes. He comes in to restore order to the society, but the society can't contain him. It's the basic idea of many Westerns – just look at *The Searchers*. It's a story form I find really useful, and I've used it a lot in various forms, even in *Trust* when the Martin Donovan character steps up to bat for society. He believes there's something wrong about the factory where he works deliberately manufacturing things badly and he makes a stand against that, which leads to him being arrested.

GF: *You talked earlier about using the Henry–Simon story as a spine to which you attach a number of ideas. These range from right-wing politics, to the uses and abuses of the Internet, to child molestation. Can you describe, in terms of the structure of the film, the relationship between the story and these ideas?*

HH: In order to sketch in this world, I wanted it to be the actual world we live in – even though it's sketched in what I think of as comic-book colors and shapes and characterization. I looked for topical things: I wanted to render that particular kind of American right-wing populist attitude that existed much more a couple of years ago than it does now. I felt the child molestation theme was pretty important and sat well with the politics. And at the time I was writing the script, there was a lot of talk about the Internet being censored. So all these things connected when I was looking for the right kind of events for these characters to be involved in – events that would render a fairly accurate picture of what America is.

GF: *It's the Warren character who espouses much of this right-wing thought, although you don't dwell on the specifics.*

HH: Right. I didn't want to get into a discussion about right-wing American politics. What was more interesting to me about Warren was the 'naive young man discovers politics' idea because he's just looking for something. This older woman he's sleeping with turns him on to this stuff, and he just gives himself to it. But he's not self-possessed enough to appreciate what politics is, so he takes it personally when the candidate loses, and he becomes cynical. I wanted to hint that I don't think there are political solutions to human problems.

GF: *It's through Henry's response to Warren's molestation of Pearl that Henry is able to exonerate himself from his past crime of statutory rape, although it's unclear whether he kills Warren because he's outraged or because Pearl has offered to pay him with oral sex. My sense of it is that Henry is simply doing a good deed out of a new-found moral outrage.*

HH: I wanted that scene in the basement between Pearl – who's aged thirteen – and Henry to be really harsh, and I wanted us to at least fear that Henry is capable of doing something stupid and horrible again. It counterbalances the scene where Henry earlier tells Simon why he went to prison. The important thing to remember there is that he claims, rather tritely I think, that this other thirteen-year-old girl he had sex with knew how to play on his weaknesses. And he admits that he's got many weaknesses, some that are profound and perverse, but he doesn't apologize for them. He doesn't even apologize for having broken the law in this way. What I find repulsive about Henry at this moment is that he feels the need to get up on the soapbox again and get into a 'woe is me' thing, which he is prone to do. But at least he claims that he did not take advantage of innocence, whereas that's exactly what Warren is doing with Pearl.

GF: *Through the course of the film, Henry is humanized – not only in the spiritual sense, but literally – as he becomes less of a symbol or an abstraction and more corporeal.*

HH: He becomes more of a recognizable human being with believable flaws. One handy phrase I used a lot during the writing was, 'What happens if the most untrustworthy man in town were the best person in town?' Henry is a completely unreliable, polymorphously perverse egomaniac, but he's a good man – the most selfless, the most honest, the most truthful, the strongest. I love telling stories like that, when people just don't fit into the box correctly.

He's willing to take advantage of opportunities, opportunities for perversion, but he's not willing to take advantage of innocence, which is, as I say, what Warren, his nemesis, does. But Henry's not even good at straightening out this problem, and he winds up getting beaten up and killing the guy. He gets progressively more pathetic, actually.

GF: *At the end of the film, Simon comes to his rescue and gets Henry to the airport before the police catch him. The final shot shows him running, but whether it's to or from the airplane isn't clear. I assumed that he's running back to Simon to face the music and be redeemed. Other people I've spoken to think he's getting the hell out of there. Want to clear this up?*

HH: I'd like to keep it open. I shot the scene with Henry running toward the plane, and then, in the editing, I discovered it was perfectly possible to keep it ambiguous and that seemed much more interesting to me. My brother was the first person to point this out to me. He saw a cut in the editing room, and when we went out for supper he said, 'Is he running toward the plane or away from it?' I went, 'How can you say that? It's so clear that he's running toward the plane,' which is the way I'd shot it geographically. My brother said, 'No, it's not.' Then we went back and looked at it and I started showing it to other people I work with. But they'd been with the film from the script stage and agreed Henry was running toward the plane. I said, 'Forget what we know. Just look at the pictures.' Then we moved some of the pictures around. There was a cutaway of an air stewardess waving Henry on. I said, 'If we got rid of that shot, it'll be completely up in the air whether he's running back toward Simon or toward the plane. Most people I've spoken to coming out of the movie don't know. They can't be certain one way or the other where he's going – and that question mark is good.

It was a big thing to deal with because you're always reaching for a particular kind of closure, and for years I had always thought Henry would be running toward the plane. But then the footage itself made this thing happen. I think it's much more poetically deep not to close it – a much more beautiful gesture.

GF: *In the shot, Henry's actually running toward us.*
HH: Yes – and we, the audience, are also outside society.

GF: *So do you yourself know the answer, or is it an open question for you, too?*
HH: It's open for me. It wasn't so hard to get rid of the presupposition that I'd been there on the tarmac and filmed him running toward the plane, and it's exciting to me when people come out of the movie and they're debating what happened.

GF: *You move the camera very sparingly in* Henry Fool. *In fact, this film is as visually essential – to use your own word – as any you've made.*
HH: The most consistent approach to making the pictures in this movie came from a question I posed myself, namely: 'What would a *cinéma verité* style look like if I wasn't allowed to move the camera, and if I used locked-off shots without overly controlling the activity in front of the lens?' The idea was to try to find an aesthetic unity without imposing my will upon the actors'

movements. I knew that I'd get pictures that could be interesting in a number of different ways. In practice, I didn't stick to this idea too often, but it did inform the entire way we made the pictures. Most of the time the camera would have its own trajectory, its own purpose, and then I would also develop a real *mise en scène* with the actors, and a lot of it would be heard but not seen. This dynamic grew out of economic concerns as much as anything else. We didn't have a lot of money.

GF: *What was the budget?*
HH: About $1 million. It's as small a film as I've made since *Trust*, but it's a much bigger film and has a lot more characters.

GF: *The camera constantly looks askance at the characters, observing them from above, below, and sometimes even from an oblique angle.*
HH: Yes. We use a lot of Dutch angles in this film. I thought I could keep the pictures alive by letting things happen off camera, and then having people intrude on the frame. I wanted to get that excitement you get in documentary, but without sacrificing the evidence of formal construction. I didn't want it to be sloppy – I wanted the images to have a strong narrative voice. By using strong, intense angles, I was trying for the clarity of style I admire in comic books, and which is more about looking than showing, although there are scenes where I had to just show – for example, when Simon and Fay's mom is found dead.

GF: *Most of the compositions are extremely tight, with an intense concentration on faces. I was particularly aware of that during the wedding sequence, where you have two set-ups of three faces at the altar. The movie is pretty claustrophobic as a result of that.*
HH: I had to reach back to a lot of creative strategies in this movie that I'd used in *The Unbelievable Truth* and *Trust*, simply because I felt the story needed to be pre-eminent. However, it was possible on occasion to stand back, look, and let the context take care of conveying other things, like Henry taking an enormous crap. You wouldn't have been aware of Fay in that shot, but I told Parker to keep going back and forth in front of the camera. Actually, it was good that we didn't see too much of her because she just couldn't keep from laughing.

I'm good at making films for very little money. It's not

something I'm particularly   re
again and that was a bit dis
performances in the scene   hen
at night and he unwittingly
that. We had no real money
black out the windows, and   he
only advantage is that the le   n
shoot each day.

GF: *The palette of* Henry Foo   e
drabness.
HH: I really just went for wh   on
things much more in *Simple*   s
thinking of *cinéma verité*, whi... I suspect is an unexpected term to
use in conjunction with my films. The thinking was, 'Let's just
look at the world and find interesting images that we can make out
of it. If I can use fewer lights, I will. If I can use less art
department stuff, I will.' Actually, what would really excite me is
to have an enormous amount of time to make a movie, and a lot
less equipment and a lot less people. That's why I've been
shooting a lot with digital video recently. With a crew of four
people you can spend a whole week shooting a ten-minute piece
and really just respond to nature. That's what I was attempting to
do in *Henry Fool*: to sculpt, to make an artifice, to strive to
construct a powerful, correct image out of what exists there. It's
not only more fun, it's more challenging creatively – and the
challenge is to not give up your aesthetic position. I feel that a lot
of movies of the past five years just haven't tried hard enough.
They have a kind of loose naturalism that they wear as a badge of
honesty, but that can be a way of not making aesthetic decisions,
of not imposing your insight on how you respond to things. It's
become like a pretense of naturalism, whereas I think a highly
formal film can be natural.

GF: *Ken Loach has said that it's much harder to make something look
real than it is to make it look stylized.*
HH: It's true – and it's a big problem. For example, trying to show
Simon throwing up on Amy's behind was very hard. In fact, I
totally fucked it up because I didn't get the key shot. I watched
gross-out movies to try and get it right and I said, 'How do they

do this stuff?' Our make-up guy said, 'Well, you definitely need a pump.' In other words, it's a stunt, and I always shy away from that kind of work because it's so hard. It's the same with sex, which I haven't shown very much of in my movies because it's so hard to pull off, especially as it's partly psychological and you've got to look after everybody's privacy.

GF: *What purpose do these Rabelaisian scenes – Simon vomiting, Henry on the john – serve for you?*

HH: I think I was trying to do exactly what Rabelais did when he said, 'Let me blast out a book where I can have an enormous amount of philosophical discussion and psychological insight in a world that's completely disgusting, and somehow the philosophy and the psychology will benefit from being rendered that way rather than if the setting was more highfalutin.' I didn't want to talk about what for me is very personal – such as criticism as a creative activity, and those other issues we've talked about – in a rarefied context. It needed to be brought to an abrasive, ugly, funny, dumb environment so, in fact, I made up lists of disgusting stuff to include.

GF: *To avoid seeming precious?*

HH: Yes, because I don't think they are precious issues; I think they're very important. I didn't want to turn people off, for example, that crucial conversation in the hallway of the hospital between Simon and Henry, by making it seem like I was intellectualizing. The sex in the garbage heap, the vomiting, the defecation – all that gets us ready to experience that conversation.

Also, I think of this Rabelaisian stuff as among the central pleasures of movie-going. I'm someone who's constantly wondering, 'Why are people going to see my movies?' or 'Why are they *not* going to see my movies but are going to others?' and I talk to people about it. And it seems people want to see sex in movies, they want to see violence, they want to see perversion. So, as an entertainer and without being cynical about it, I thought, 'How can I make the kind of movie I want to make and still provide these things?' My starting places are my real interest in people and my sense of humor, so I certainly won't be making a gangster movie where unknown faces get swatted indiscriminately. I'll try to fit the violence, the sex, the grossness into my world.

GF: *It's as unexpected in* Henry Fool *as the shootings in* Amateur.

HH: Yes, and it comes more fast and furiously. I think I wanted to signal to the audience right at the beginning, 'Loosen up, we're going to have a lot of unexpected disgustingness.'

GF: Henry Fool *might be described as a 'problem film,' in the same way that we speak of Shakespeare's 'problem plays.' You don't spoon-feed the audience easy answers or a protagonist with whom it's that easy to empathize.*

HH: This is a movie that was made in the writing, more so than anything since *Trust*. I wrote it and then went out and made pictures of it. And in the writing there's a careful calculation about the viewer's emotional response. You think, 'Am I supposed to like Henry now? He's disgusting. But if I admit it to myself, his disgustingness is really entertaining.' But then five minutes later he'll do something like tell Simon he was sent to prison for having sex with a thirteen-year-old girl. So, yes, it's a problem. The film wants the audience to be thinking constantly about why it either likes or dislikes Henry at that point, so ultimately, hopefully, when he's in the basement with Pearl, there is real tension – and maybe some suspicion that he's dumb enough to commit the same crime again.

GF: *At this stage in your career, do you think that you're consolidating your themes and interests and style, or are you ready to go in different directions?*

HH: I'm always aware of boiling down – maybe not the themes, but certainly the ways of working. I'm always striving for poetic economy, which seems to me to be a specific thing. More broadly, I'm interested in moving out to a degree, to try to make different kinds of movies in different ways. But I think I'll always strive for something I – and people like me – have inherited from Robert Bresson more than anyone else: economy of gesture and economy in conveying meaning. To me, that's what's constantly interesting about this medium.

NOTE

This is the original screenplay. It contains scenes that are not in the finished film, and in some cases the order of scenes has changed.

Henry Fool

EXT. JUNK YARD – DAY

A garbage truck roars by and . . .

Simon Grim hangs from the back of it. He is a shy, skinny and terrified-looking guy around thirty years old.

The truck rumbles to a halt and Simon climbs down off it to go punch out at the time clock.

EXT. BEHIND THE WORLD OF DONUTS – DAY

Moments later.

He comes walking up a small alley and sits to drink his beer.

He begins to relax. This is his quality private time.

Then he hears something and looks up.

He peeks up over the edge of some junked kitchen appliances and sees . . .

Two teenage kids – Warren and Amy – smoking crack and having sex.

Simon looks on, intrigued, as Warren smokes, then . . .

> WARREN
> (*to Amy*)

You want some?

Amy takes the pipe and smokes as he feels her up.

Simon is fascinated. He drinks and looks on as . . .

Amy grins up foolishly at Warren and lowers the pipe. The boy undoes his belt and hikes up the girl's skirt.

Simon can't believe this. He looks around to see if the coast is clear, then returns just in time to see . . .

3

Warren take Amy by the waist and enter her.

The pipe falls from the young girl's hand.

Warren throws his head back and grinds himself into her.

Simon's mouth falls open in awe.

But Amy tosses her head back to the side and sees . . .

The amazed garbage man; caught.

Amy starts screaming insanely.

Simon runs for his life.

Amy and Warren throw rocks and bottles at him as they chase him away.

INT. THE GRIM HOUSE – DAY

Moments later.

Simon runs up and throws open the screen door. He stands there in the doorway catching his breath.

His sister, Fay, is at the kitchen table watching a small portable TV while their mother, Mary, sits a few feet away in the living-room watching another TV tuned to a different channel.

                    FAY
                (to Simon)
    Where the hell have you been?
                (to Mary)
    Mom, come on and eat.

                    MARY
    I'm not hungry.

                    FAY
                (pissed)
    Then why'd I cook!

Mary is a manic-depressive, still in her bathrobe at six in the evening.

MARY

I don't know why you cooked! I don't know why you bother!

Fay holds her head in her hands and sighs. She glares at her brother.

FAY

Sit down and eat, Simon.

Simon sits at the table and Fay slams down before him a bowl of some sort of gruel. He hesitates, then lifts his spoon. Supper is horrible and he screws up his face in disgust. Fay gives him a sideways glance and he leans back down over the bowl and eats some more.

Pushing the bowl away gently, he reaches out for the container of milk on the table and drinks straight from it.

He suddenly jumps back and spits out sour milk all over the table. The container drops to the floor and thick globs of cheese roll out.

He stands back against the fridge, holding his stomach while . . .

Fay and Mary look on in disgust.

EXT. THE GRIM HOUSE – DAY

Moments later.

Simon crosses the lawn and sits on the curb outside his house. He stares at the ground before him as he holds his stomach and spits, sickened.

He looks up, though, and sees . . .

A little seven-year-old girl – Pearl age seven – standing there in the street watching him.

Simon tries to smile at her.

But she throws a rock at him and hits him in the head.

He falls forward, hurt, as the little girl runs away. Lowering his hand, he sees he's bleeding. Desperate, lonely and ill, he drags his bloodied fingers across the coarse pavement.

Fay slams out of the side door of the house in a tight-fitting dress and stands on the lawn, applying lipstick.

God, I wanna get fucked.

Fay snaps shut her compact, straightens her skirt and sighs.

You OK?

Simon loses track of what he is hearing and relaxes. He looks back at his sister.

Fay fluffs out her hair and walks off.

See ya later.

Simon watches her go, but is still drawn to something he seems to hear up the street in the other direction. He cocks his head, sits perfectly still and listens.

He hears it now. We do, too. Footsteps. Big ones. Like a giant somewhere in the distance. The neighborhood trembles.

Titles begin.

Simon tries to figure out where it's coming from; the sky, the house, the highway at the end of his block . . . Finally, he focuses on . . .

The blacktop right before him, smeared with his own blood.

Music starts.

He kneels out slowly into the street and stares at the pavement. He stretches out his hand and places it flat on the road.

The pounding is louder now, becoming the beat of the music over the scene.

Simon lowers his face to the pavement, closes his eyes and . . .

Puts his ear right down against the road. He hears . . .

The steady tread of somebody very much larger than life.

Kneeling forward, with his ear to the ground, Simon opens his eyes and sees . . .

A man approaching. The music swells up full.

Simon lifts his head slowly from the road, looking off in wonder at . . .

This stranger coming towards him; an oddly handsome freak striding over the crest of the distant intersection with a windswept mane, two over-stuffed suitcases and a crumpled tie fluttering back over his broad but crooked shoulders.

Simon rises till he's kneeling up straight in the road.

Henry Fool finally reaches him and stops.

Titles finish.

Simon says nothing and watches as Henry looks off at the house.

Satisfied, but wary, Henry Fool looks around the neighborhood and then down at Simon.

HENRY

Get up off your knees.

He tosses the suitcases down in front of Simon and walks off towards his new home.

EXT. BACK OF THE GRIM HOUSE – DAY

Henry comes around behind the house and finds the door to his basement apartment. He approaches. Simon follows, carrying the suitcases.

INT. HENRY'S APARTMENT – DAY

Moments later.

The door is wrenched open and Henry is hit square in the jaw by a decade of dank airless gloom. He coughs.

Entering, he finds a few old wooden chairs littering the main room. He inspects the old wood stove, then takes a chair and smashes it. He tosses the wood in the stove.

Simon looks on, amazed. Henry lights a fire with unusually quick results, then stands back and looks at Simon.

> HENRY
> Where you gotta go to get a six-pack of beer around here?

INT. WORLD OF DONUTS – DAY

This is a convenience store with a number of tables at which to eat donuts.

Warren is shoplifting while Amy terrorizes Gnoc Deng, the Vietnamese cashier, who stares out at them from behind the safety of the counter.

> AMY
> Say something.

> WARREN
> (*calling*)
> She's mute.

> AMY
> What?

> WARREN
> She don't – you know – talk.

Amy looks back at Gnoc, snarls, then follows the cashier's gaze to the door.

Simon enters. Clutching Henry's cash, he stops dead in his tracks when he sees . . .

Warren and Amy.

He steps forward and approaches the beer cooler.

Warren and Amy hover around, just out of reach, like a couple of vampires.

Dragging a six-pack out of the cooler, Simon crosses to the counter. Warren and Amy hang back, silent and threatening.

Gnoc rings up the purchase and glances over at . . .

Amy, staring a hole into the side of Simon's skull.

Gnoc hands Simon back his change and he makes for the door, but . . .

Warren shoves himself between it and Simon.

Simon freezes. Warren is expressionless. Simon looks back at Amy. She turns away, reaches up under her skirt, jerks down her panties, then leans forward on to the counter. Leering back over her shoulder, she hisses . . .

AMY

Kiss my ass.

Simon is nonplussed.

Gnoc presses a button on the wall that sets . . .

A red light flashing above the stockroom door.

Warren grabs Simon by the neck and drags him over to Amy's bare behind. Amy laughs as Simon is forced to his knees and has his face shoved up right into the crack of her ass.

But then . . . Simon throws up all over her.

Warren falls back in disgust.

Gnoc covers her face with her hands.

Amy looks around at herself, realizes, and starts screaming bloody murder.

Simon falls back on to the floor, clutching his stomach, as Amy staggers around with her vomit-strewn underwear down around her ankles.

Then Gnoc's father, Mr Deng, appears at the stockroom door holding a shovel and ready to fight.

(*scared*)

Oh, shit!

Mr Deng comes running at them and Warren drags Amy from the store. Simon crawls out of the way as the old man throws open the door to the parking lot and screams at the retreating delinquents . . .

MR DENG
(*in Vietnamese*)
Stay the hell out of my store, you good-for-nothing punks!

Having scared them off, he comes back in and starts screaming at Simon.

Look at this! What's going on here? Simon, get up off the floor! Is this beer paid for?

INT. HENRY'S APARTMENT – NIGHT

Later.

Simon splashes water over his face at the kitchen sink, then watches as Henry unpacks one of his suitcases. It is filled with dozens of old, worn notebooks. Henry stacks them on the mantelpiece over the fireplace; the fire is now crackling and bright.

Simon steps over and looks at . . .

The name tag on the other suitcase: 'Henry Fool'.

HENRY
(*off-screen*)

Centuries ago it had an 'e' at the end.

Simon looks over and sees . . .

Henry's silhouette against the fire. He steps forward into the light and grabs a beer from the six-pack on the floor. He hands one to Simon.

Simon takes it and stares at it a moment before raising his eyes to Henry.

SIMON

Where do you come from?

HENRY

Nowhere in particular.

He winks at Simon, then struts around the room, hugely impressed with himself.

I go where I will and I do what I must.
(*stops, drinks*)
That's why I'm in trouble. I'm sort've what you might call
. . . 'in exile'.

SIMON

Why are you in trouble?

HENRY
(*stopping*)

An honest man is always in trouble, Simon. Remember that.

Simon comes away from the fire, watching him carefully. Henry stands in a dim corner across the room.

SIMON

How do you know my name?

Henry pauses, looks aside, drinks, then grins demoniacally. He steps forward and comes face to face with Simon. He lifts his finger and points to . . .

Simon's name stitched upon the breast of his work shirt.

Realizing this, Simon moves off and thinks.

Henry throws more wood on the fire, glancing back over his shoulder, laughing mischievously.

> SIMON
> (*stopping him*)
>
> I am not retarded.

> HENRY
> (*pauses*)
>
> Well . . . I'll take your word for that.

> SIMON
> (*explaining*)
>
> People. I mean. They think. You know. Because.

He tries to articulate what he thinks he feels but winds up gesticulating curiously with his hands. This finally dissolves into a dumb stare into empty space.

> HENRY
>
> I see.

Simon looks at him. Henry stands and grabs a notebook from off the mantelpiece. He tears out a few pages and shoves them in his pocket. He hands the now fresh writing tablet to Simon.

> Here. Take this. And . . .

He searches his pockets and finds a pencil.

> . . . this. Keep them with you at all times. You ever feel like you got something to say and you can't get it out, stop and write it down. OK?

Simon hesitates, then accepts the gifts. Henry goes for another beer while his new friend studies the dozens of notebooks on the mantelpiece.

> SIMON
>
> What are these?

HENRY
(*proudly, returning*)
This? This is my life's work. My memoirs. My 'Confession'.

SIMON
(*carefully*)
What have you done?

Henry drinks and looks down into the raging fire.

HENRY
(*wistfully*)
I've been bad. Repeatedly.
(*shrugs and steps away*)
But why brag? The details of my exploits are only a pretext for
a far more expansive consideration of general truths.
(*contemplating the notebooks*)
What is this? It's a philosophy. A poetics. A politics, if you
will. A literature of protest. A novel of ideas. A pornographic
magazine of truly comic-book proportions. It is, in the end,
whatever the hell I want it to be. And when I'm through with
it, it's gunna blow a hole *this wide* straight through the world's
own idea of itself!

*He smokes. Simon is impressed. They hear a bottle smash outside in the
street and Henry goes to the window.*

They're throwing bottles at the house.
(*throwing down his cigarette*)
Come on, let's go break their arms!

Simon jumps up.

SIMON
No!

Henry stops. Simon looks away and sits back down.

(*pauses*)

If I'm quiet.

He is ashamed of himself.

Henry sees this and settles down. He considers his new friend with

13

genuine care as he gets himself a new cigarette. He lights up, thinks,
then grabs another chair and sits close by Simon. They sit there in
silence a while, then . . .

                    HENRY
Once. I forget where I was. Central America maybe.
Somewhere hot. Stupid job. Bad pay. Dangerous location
and water so foul the natives wouldn't even piss in it. This
crowd of drunken motherfuckers hired by the local drug
cartel shows up at my hotel room and threatens to tear me
limb from limb. And I say, listen, *hombres*, OK, you've got me
outnumbered four to one and you're gunna kill me here
tonight and not a soul in this dimly lit world is ever gunna
notice I'm gone. Fine. But one of you . . . one of you . . . one
of you is gunna have his eye torn out. Period. Silence. I repeat
myself. One of you poor, underpaid jerks is gunna have an
eye ripped out of its socket. I promise. It's a small thing,
perhaps, all things considered. But I will succeed. Because it's
the only thing I have left to do in this world. So why don't
you just take a good look at one another one last time and
think it over for a few minutes more.
                    (*smokes, waits*)
They sober up a little, look at their shoes in confusion, then
step out into the hall to talk among themselves.

Henry stares into the flames and falls silent. Simon is riveted. He leans
forward, on the edge of his seat . . .

                    SIMON
What happened?

                    HENRY
                    (*winking*)
Well, here I am, still, after all.

INT. THE GRIM HOUSE. UPSTAIRS – NIGHT

Later that night.

Simon climbs the stairs and stops when he hears raunchy sex from his
sister's room. He stands outside her door and listens.

MARY
(*off*)
Did you throw up all over some girl?

Simon looks up the hall and sees his mother in her room, sitting on the edge of her bed, smoking. He approaches and stands in her doorway.

They were throwing bottles at the house.

Simon says nothing. He looks down at his feet.

(*gesturing to Fay's room*)
She's got some ex-con in there she met at the bar. Tattoos all over himself and a big red bloated nose.

SIMON
Did you take your pills?

Now she says nothing. She smokes and looks away.

Simon steps into the bathroom and gets her medication. He runs a glass of water and brings it in to her.

She swallows the pills and washes them back with water.

You want me to tell her to be quiet?

She looks away, unconcerned and cynical.

MARY
What's the use? She might as well get it while she can. She's not always gunna have the ass she has now, you know. That's just how life is.

She throws the blanket over herself and turns off the light. Simon stands there in the dark.

INT. THE GRIM HOUSE KITCHEN – NIGHT

Moments later.

Simon comes downstairs into the quiet, dark kitchen and sits at the table. He listens to the traffic on the highway and stares off into space. Finally, he takes the notebook Henry gave him from his pocket and places it before him. But then he just gazes off into the dim living-room and scratches his head. Returning his attention to the notebook, he digs down into his pocket and retrieves his short stub of pencil.

He opens the notebook and carefully flattens back the cover. Lifting the pencil, he pauses and stares at the blank page. Then, after more intense hesitation, he brings the pencil's dull tip to the very top left edge of the page and begins writing in a slow, laborious hand.

INT. THE GRIM HOUSE KITCHEN – DAY

The next morning.

Henry barges in the kitchen door with two containers of coffee and some jelly donuts. Simon jumps up from where he sits asleep over his notebook at the table.

> HENRY
> Good morning, Simon! Glorious day, huh? Here, have a donut. Can you lend me twenty dollars?

Simon rubs the sleep from his eyes, blinks, disoriented and reaches for his wallet.

> Thanks. Where's the library in the scruffy little burgh?

> SIMON
> *(handing him cash)*
> Down the highway about a mile and a half and then make a left.

> HENRY
> Excellent! I'm polishing up the final chapters of my 'Confession' and I need a reasonably well-stocked reference section.

He lifts up Simon's notebook.

> What's this?

Simon hesitates, shyly.

> SIMON
> I thought. Um. I was. I wanted to. Maybe.

He gives up, sighs and gazes at the floor. Henry flips through the book,

impressed. It is full from cover to cover, every page dense with Simon's cryptic scrawl. Henry frowns, intrigued. Then . . .

HENRY

Can I take this?

Simon looks up, terrified. But his friend puts him at ease.

I'll correct the spelling.

EXT. JUNK YARD – DAY

Later that day.

Simon finds a number of volumes of the classics while crushing garbage.

EXT. BEHIND WORLD OF DONUTS – DAY

That evening.

Simon sits with his evening beer and his new collection of soiled classics. He cracks open a volume of Shakespeare and tries to read. It's an obvious struggle. He puts it aside and lifts up Wordsworth, studying its cover and the texture of the pages. A page flutters away and he climbs down to the edge of a greasy puddle to retrieve it. It's now wet and torn, so he flattens it out on the concrete and tries to fit it back into the book.

He reads a little, furrowing his brow, then drinks. He bites his lip and tries again.

He sits back, exhausted and thinks. He hears a twig snap and looks back over his shoulder to see . . .

Amy throws a bottle at his head.

Smash!!!! He falls to the ground, blood streaming down his neck.

Warren runs over and grabs him by the shirt, lifting him out of the puddle and smacking him in the head.

Amy runs forward and waits with a rolled-up newspaper which she sets aflame with her lighter.

Warren punches Simon in the stomach and throws him to the ground, then unzips his fly and pisses on him.

Amy watches, giggling excitedly, waving the flaming torch.

Simon crawls away and grabs hold of an old section of fence, while Warren zips up and grabs the fire from Amy.

Simon pulls himself to his knees, rests his face against the rusted fence and gasps for breath. Warren waves the flaming torch in his face.

(*weakly, unheard*)
One of you is gunna lose an eye.

Amy comes nearer with a can of gasoline. Simon pulls himself to his feet as she splashes him with fuel. Warren is waving the torch deliriously above his head.

(*screaming*)
One of you is gunna lose an eye!

Warren stops.

Amy steps back and lowers the gas can.

Simon turns with effort to face them, adjusts his glasses and continues . . .

One of you. I promise.

Warren watches him blankly, then is burned by the torch which is too hot to handle. He drops it.

Amy giggles, then stops, excited, but confused.

Simon grips the rusted chainlink so that it cuts into his hands and stares straight at Warren.

You can set me on fire. But one of you is gunna have an eye torn out of your head. I promise.

Warren is transfixed. He shivers and looks at Amy, who steps back, scared, and puts down the gas can. She turns and walks away.

Warren looks back at Simon, troubled.

He hangs there still, glaring at him.

Further away, Warren rejoins Amy and stares at his hands. Amy looks ill.

WARREN
Fuck.

AMY
Take me home.

INT. WORLD OF DONUTS – DAY

Henry is at one of the tables, correcting the spelling in Simon's notebook, when he looks up and sees . . .

Simon stumble in, beaten and bruised, dropping his classics to the floor. Henry and Mr Deng rush over to him.

> HENRY
> (*scared*)
> Simon! Who did this to you?

> SIMON
> I was gunna tear out their eyes. I knew I could do it.

> HENRY
> Whose eyes?

> SIMON
> I told them. Like you said. I told them. And I knew I could do it.

He passes out. Henry looks at Mr Deng.

> MR DENG
> You should take him home. He smells like a toilet.

Henry nods, agreeing, then lifts Simon off the floor. Mr Deng holds the door open as Henry carries his friend out into the parking lot.

Meanwhile, Gnoc gathers up the classics from the floor and places them beside Simon's notebook, where it still sits open on the table. She looks at it, then reads. She lifts it off the table and reads further, immediately and deeply engrossed.

Mr Deng watches as Henry departs with Simon, then comes back into the store and stops, startled, when he sees . . .

Gnoc sitting there, staring off into space, the notebook open in her hands before her, singing quietly.

INT. THE GRIM HOUSE – DAY

Twenty minutes later.

Fay is in the bathroom helping Simon out of his clothes, trying to clean his wounds.

> FAY
> (*calling*)
> Shit, Mom, we gotta get him to a hospital!

> SIMON
> No!

> FAY
> Oh, shut up! Turn around.

Henry is at the kitchen table with Mary. She watches him suspiciously. He lets her.

> MARY
> This kinda thing has happened before.

> HENRY
> (*standing*)
> It won't happen again.

She watches him as he walks around the room, browsing.

> MARY
> How do you know?

He stops and lifts a small framed photo of a soldier off the piano.

HENRY

This your husband?

Violated somehow, she gets up and snatches it out of his hands. She puts it in a drawer and cringes as Henry plays one note on the piano.

MARY

Stop that.

He fixes her with a steady, knowing stare which causes her to gather the collar of her bathrobe up around her neck. She steps back, exposed, when there's a knock at the door. They look over to see . . .

Mr Deng enter with the notebook.

MR DENG
(nods to Mary, then)

Mr Fool, what is this?

HENRY

It's poetry.

MR DENG

Are you sure?

Henry comes over, takes the notebook from him and shoves it in his pocket.

HENRY

Of course I'm sure. I corrected the spelling myself.

MR DENG

It made my daughter sing.

HENRY

Yeah, well, you know – that's what poetry does.

MR DENG

But she has never spoken in her life.

Meanwhile, back in the bathroom . . .

SIMON

Owww!!!

FAY

Keep still!

SIMON

Let me do it!

FAY
(*fed up*)
Fine! You do it, Simon! I don't care!

She storms out to the top of the stairs, cocks her hip and whines . . .

Mom! Simon's got a broken rib, his shoulder's dislocated or something, and he won't let me disinfect the gash in his head!

MARY
Fay, just take him to the hospital, will ya!

FAY
(*stamping her foot*)
But he won't go!

MARY
(*screaming*)
Simon Grim, you go to the hospital with Fay right now, do hear me!

Simon reaches out and slams the bathroom door.

Fay looks from the bathroom door down the stairs to Mary. Mary, her nerves rattled, glances over at Mr Deng, who turns and leaves the house.

Henry lights a fresh cigarette, loosens his tie and heads upstairs.

INT. THE GRIM HOUSE BATHROOM – DAY

A moment later.

Henry throws open the door and enters. He steps over Simon, who is on the floor, folded up against the toilet.

HENRY
We gotta talk.

Henry sits on the edge of the bathtub and takes the notebook from his pocket.

23

What the hell were you trying to do when you wrote this
thing?

Simon just looks at him, not certain what he means.

SIMON

Nothing.

HENRY

Well, you know you wrote it in a kind of iambic pentameter.

SIMON

Iambic what?

HENRY

Verse.

He scratches his chin and smokes.

Look, in my opinion, this is pretty powerful stuff. Though
your spelling is Neanderthal, and your reasoning a little naive,
your instincts are profound. But the whole thing needs to be
given a more cohesive shape. It can be expanded. Followed
through. Unified.
(*smokes, then*)
You see what I'm getting at?

*Simon just stares at him, overwhelmed. Henry drops the notebook on
the floor and points at it with his cigarette.*

Are you willing to commit yourself to this? To really work on
it? To give it its due? In the face of adversity and
discouragement? To rise to the challenge you yourself have
set?

Simon just blinks, looks away and wonders.

And don't gimme that wonderstruck 'I'm-only-a-humble-
garbage-man' bullshit, either.

SIMON

It hurts to breathe.

                              HENRY
                             (*nodding*)
Of course it does.

Simon coughs and Henry leans back and smokes.

INT. THE GRIM HOUSE UPSTAIRS – NIGHT

An hour later

*Fay cringes outside Simon's room as Henry goes about setting her
brother's arm.*

                              SIMON
Like this?

                              HENRY
Yeah. No. OK?

                              SIMON
Wait!

                              HENRY
Don't move! Fuck. There.

                              SIMON
Are you sure that's right?

                              HENRY
Yes. Now shut up and lie back.

Simon does.

                              SIMON
Is this gunna hurt?

                              HENRY
Yes.

He pauses, then leans back.

You gunna be alright?

Simon nods and stares at the ceiling. Henry hands him a towel.

HENRY

Here. Bite on this.

SIMON
(*spots blood on it*)

What's that?

HENRY
(*looking*)

It's blood. From your head. Lie back. Shove that in your mouth and hold on to something.

Simon bites down on the towel and grips the edge of the bed with his free hand. Henry sits on his legs and gently raises the broken arm.

Outside the door, Fay bites her knuckles. Further down the hall, Mary listens from her bedroom.

Okay. You ready?

Simon nods. Henry grabs hold of the arm, swallows and braces himself. Simon waits, then Henry tugs the arm straight.

SIMON

Aaagghhh!!!!!!!

Fay turns and runs down the stairs. Mary backs away into her room and shuts the door.

INT. THE GRIM HOUSE KITCHEN – NIGHT

Later that night.

Henry comes downstairs and stops, tired. Fay is sitting at the table with a bottle of gin and two glasses. She has dolled herself up a little and Henry likes what he sees. He looks her over and she smiles. He sits. She pours. They drink.

FAY

So, do you have, like, you know, a girlfriend, Henry?

HENRY

No.

They drink again in silence. He lights her cigarette and they watch each other closely. Finally, Fay leans on the table and twirls a strand of her hair between her fingers.

FAY

Do you find me attractive?

HENRY

Yes, I do.

FAY

I look young for my age, don't I?

HENRY

How old are you?

FAY

How old do you think I am?

HENRY

You look young.

FAY
(*playfully*)

How young?

HENRY

I don't know. Young.

FAY

But how . . . I mean, do I look more like twenty, or . . . you know, thirty?

He drinks and studies her. She presents her profile. Finally, he leans back.

HENRY

Thirty.

Fay jumps up, furious.

FAY

Listen, you geek, after a couple of drinks plenty of people mistake me for eighteen!

She grabs her bag and storms out of the house. Henry watches her go, then chuckles deviously and splashes himself another drink.

EXT. WORLD OF DONUTS – DAY

Next morning.

A thirty-year-old cocktail waitress named Vicky walks up and stops when she sees . . .

Warren, sitting back against the side of World of Donuts, smoking a joint and thinking about his future.

She sighs and approaches.

>   VICKY
> Hey, Warren, are you a registered voter?

>   WARREN
> Bug off, Vicky!

Unruffled, she hands him a flyer.

>   (reading)
> 'Saving America From Itself.' What the fuck is this?

>   VICKY
> It's everything you need to know about the upcoming
> elections and congressman Owen Feer and all the really good
> things he wants to do for our country.

He tokes deeply, then . . .

>   WARREN
> Oh yeah, like what?

>   VICKY
> He wants to win back this country for us Americans, Warren,
> and restore some kind of cultural-moral standard to our way
> of life.

Warren looks over the flyer, then reconsiders Vicky.

>   WARREN
> What time's your kid go off to school?

                        VICKY
                     (*carefully*)
Nine o'clock.

                        WARREN
How about I come over and visit you later?

Vicky sighs, troubled. She adjusts her waitress uniform and looks mildly offended.

                        VICKY
Well, I don't know, Warren. I mean . . .

Warren gets up, too.

                        WARREN
Come on. I mean it. I'm trying to change.

Vicky is hard-pressed. She wants to believe him, but knows better. She thinks about it while . . .

Henry passes by and approaches the store.

INT. WORLD OF DONUTS – DAY

Same time.

Henry enters and takes Simon's notebook from his pocket. He flips through a few pages and selects one in particular.

He tears it out of the book and tapes it up beside the register so customers can read it. He winks at Gnoc. She smiles shyly and makes him a coffee. He takes it and moves off to a table just as . . .

Vicky enters. She starts accumulating groceries, placing them on the counter one item at a time.

Henry settles down and watches as . . .

Vicky returns to the counter with a bottle of orange juice and notices the poem. She reads, holding the orange juice out to her side.

Gnoc starts to ring up the other purchases as her father comes up behind her, busying himself with an inventory of the cigarettes.

Vicky's lip starts to tremble as she reads, a horrified expression clouding her face. Finally . . .

Smash!!!! She drops the bottle of orange juice and stands back. Mr Deng and Gnoc jump back, alarmed.

Henry tilts his head and pays close attention.

VICKY
(screaming at Mr Deng)

How dare you put something like this up where anyone can see it!

Mr Deng looks from her to the poem and then over at Henry. Henry urges the man to stand up for himself.

MR DENG
(to Vicky)

It's poetry.

VICKY

It's pornography! The product of a diseased mind! You oughta be ashamed of yourself, Mr Deng!

MR DENG

It made Gnoc sing.

30

VICKY
(*pauses, confused*)
It's disgusting! There oughta be a law or something!

She grabs her things and leaves. Mr Deng holds his head and looks over at Henry.

HENRY
(*winking*)
There's no accounting for taste, is there, Mr Deng?

Mr Deng has no idea. He sits, worried, as Gnoc comes out from behind the counter and begins mopping up the mess.

INT. THE GRIM HOUSE KITCHEN – DAY

Later.

Henry is at the kitchen table with Simon, working on the poem. Simon is bandaged up, his arm in a sling, black eyes, etc.

HENRY
See, Simon, there are three kinds of there. There's 'There'. T-H-E-R-E. There are the donuts. Then there's T-H-E-I-R; which is the possessive. It is their donut. Then, finally, there's 'they're'. T-H-E-Y-'-R-E. A contraction, meaning they are. They're the donut people. Get it?

SIMON
Uh-huh.

Henry lifts up one of Simon's newly acquired classics . . .

HENRY
And look, if you're gunna read Wordsworth you've gotta get a more up-to-date edition. This odoriferous tome you're so attached to doesn't even have all fourteen books of the *Prelude*. And you need notes. Commentary. I'll go to the library and find you the best edition they have.

SIMON
Thank you, but that's OK. I'll stop there on my way back from work.

                         HENRY
From work? You can't go to work.

                         SIMON
Well, yes, maybe not today, but, you know, tomorrow,
probably.

                         HENRY
Quit.

                         SIMON
My job?

                         HENRY
Yeah.

                         SIMON
Why?

                         HENRY
You need time to write, Simon. To study. To reflect.

                         SIMON
But I like my job.

                         HENRY
We all have to make sacrifices. A vocation like ours, Simon, is
not a nine to five thing. You can't put a fence around a man's
soul. We think and feel where and when we can think and
feel. We are the servants of our muse and we toil where she
commands.

Simon looks past him and Henry follows his gaze to find . . .

*Mary standing at the foot of the stairs, listening to them. She says
nothing. She looks Henry up and down, then shakes her head
disdainfully and grunts. She throws herself on the couch and turns on
the TV, casting acid glances over at the kitchen.*

EXT. THE GRIM HOUSE – DAY

Moments later.

Henry and Simon come outside . . .

HENRY

Your mom's got a bad attitude, Simon.

SIMON

She's clinically depressed.

HENRY

Yeah, and what's that mean?

SIMON
(*thinking, then*)
I guess it means it's not her fault.

Henry wanders out to the road, checking his wallet, then . . .

HENRY
(*sighing*)
You ever think of leaving?

SIMON

Here?

HENRY

Yeah.

SIMON

To go where?

HENRY

Out there. You know, into the world. Where ever.

Simon looks off, thinks it over and slowly nods.

SIMON

Yeah, I guess.

HENRY
(*reciting*)
'Opportunity will step away and make room for a man to pass
it by.'

SIMON

Is that from your book?

HENRY

No. I found it in a fortune cookie.

He pulls the tiny piece of crumpled advice out from one of his pockets and shows it to Simon.

> SIMON
>
> Can I read your confession?

> HENRY
>
> No. Not yet. Soon. We'll see.

> SIMON
>
> Is it almost finished?

> HENRY
> (*puffing himself up*)
>
> Well, you know, Simon, a piece of work like this, it's . . . A vocation like ours . . . You can't put a fence around a man's soul. What I'm trying to achieve, it's . . . Well, it takes a lifetime really. It's a life's work.
> (*looking around*)
>
> But soon. Don't worry. I'd appreciate your feedback. I gotta go. See ya.

He hurries away around the corner. Simon walks back to the house and stops when he sees . . .

A plain-clothes policeman, Officer Buñuel, drive up and park before the house.

Simon spies as the man gets out of his car and knocks on Henry's door. He, of course, gets no answer.

INT. THE GRIM HOUSE KITCHEN – DAY

Later that day.

Simon works on his poem at the kitchen table while Fay flips through a magazine and watches TV. Mary, lying on the couch in her bathrobe, watches her own TV.

The cacophony is augmented by the rattling dishwasher and the trucks rumbling by on the highway outside.

Mary looks over at her son, suspicious, and leans off the couch.

MARY

What are you doing there, Simon?

He carefully finishes writing a word, then looks up and pauses.

SIMON

I'm writing a poem.

Mary looks at Fay, who looks up from her magazine and considers her brother. Then they break out laughing.

Simon looks on.

They laugh and laugh and laugh . . .

INT. WORLD OF DONUTS – DAY

Later.

Simon is bent over his notebook, consulting a dictionary, hard at work.

Amy and three kids are grouped around the register, reading the page Henry taped up earlier. As they read, Amy glances anxiously back at Simon.

They finish reading and stand back.

PAT

So what? It ain't so great.

CHRIS
(*to Amy, of Simon*)

That him?

Amy nods 'Yes', then leads them towards Simon.

Simon scribbles away.

AMY
(*off*)

Pardon me, Simon.

He looks up, sees her, panics and slides away on the seat. Amy looks down and bites her lip, contrite. She sighs.

Uhm. Look, ah . . . I'm the editor of the high school newspaper now and . . .

PAT

One of the editors.

AMY

One of the editors, and we . . .

PAT

You.

AMY

I . . . wanted to know if we could print your poem in this month's issue.

Simon looks around at them all, threatened.

SIMON

Why?

AMY

Because I think it's great.

PAT

I don't.

CHRIS
(*to Pat*)

Who cares what you think?

TED

You're a drag.

CHRIS

A well-known drag.

AMY
(*to Simon*)

Please?

Simon fumbles with his pencil, ill at ease and self-conscious. Then, to get rid of them, he nods his consent.

INT. THE GRIM HOUSE – DAY

That evening.

Fay comes downstairs in only a towel and wet hair. She switches on the

TV and looks for cigarettes. She finds Mary's pills on the table and remembers to ask . . .

FAY

Ma, you take your medication?

Mary is lying on the couch. She drags her eyes from the TV and glances lazily at Fay, then back to the TV.

(*to herself*)

Guess so.

She sits at the kitchen table and lifts her magazine.

Henry shows up at the kitchen door with a pile of library books. His eyes brighten when he sees . . .

Fay sitting there wearing only her towel. He knocks. She looks back over her shoulder and sees him.

HENRY

Evening, Fay.

FAY
(*disdainfully*)

What do you want?

HENRY

I've got these books for Simon.

She turns away.

FAY

Well, leave 'em there on the counter, then.

He comes in and stacks the books near the sink. Fay pretends to ignore him, but rakes her fingers through her wet hair anyway, to show more shoulder.

This is not lost on Henry, who tarries and leans back against the counter, salivating.

Fay flips through her magazine and Henry steps closer and leans against the fridge.

She casts a bored glance in his direction, then returns her attention to the TV. She senses him step aside and follows his movements without turning. Suddenly his hand appears from behind her and gently strokes her hair. She freezes, waits, wonders . . .

He leans his face down beside her. She looks at him. He looks at her, then down to . . .

Her bare legs crossed before her on the kitchen chair. His hand moves down and slides itself deep in between her thighs.

Her mouth drops open.

He looks back up at her. He grins.

Fay jumps up and away, breathlessly clutching the towel around herself.

Henry casts a glance over her body, throws his hair back out of his face and shivers with lust.

Fay steps back and grabs hold of the staircase banister, making an unconvincing gesture of injured pride.

Henry comes closer and she steps backwards up the stairs.

He stops, loosens his tie, holding her with his gaze.

She readjusts her towel, throws back her wet hair, sighs defiantly, then sashays into her room, leaving the door ajar.

Henry waits there at the foot of the stairs, reaches down, grabs his crotch and repositions his hard-on. He takes a step up the stairs, then stops. He looks over to the couch and sees . . .

Mary, lying there, sedately amazed.

He pauses, then grins.

Mary blinks and smiles sleepily.

INT. WORLD OF DONUTS – DAY

Same time.

Simon sits back from his writing and rubs his neck. Putting down his pencil, he looks up and sees . . .

Warren enter the store and grab a beer from the cooler. Seeing Simon, he waves and approaches.

> WARREN

Hey, Simon, you a registered voter?

Simon hesitates, but then nods uncertainly. Warren hands him a flyer.

This year when you go to the polls, I want you to consider Congressman Owen Feer. He wants to restore America to its position of unmatched wealth, power and opportunity; to revitalize American civilization and lead the human race to even greater levels of freedom, prosperity and security! He's a good man.

He steps over to the register and pays for his beer. Mr Deng glares at him, distrustfully. Warren stops on his way out and snarls at the old man . . .

Immigrant.

He leaves. Simon looks down and studies the flyer.

INT. THE GRIM HOUSE. UPSTAIRS – DAY

Same time.

Fay lies across her bed in her towel, holding a pose and glancing anxiously back at the door. Finally, losing her patience, she gets up.

FAY

Where is he?

She opens the door and looks out into the hall.

He's not there.

She steps out into the hall and listens.

Henry?

Nothing. She comes to the top of the stairs and hears faint activity from down below. She proceeds downstairs.

She sees no one in the kitchen, then looks in the living-room and stops. She goes white, her mouth falling open in horror.

Henry and Mary are screwing one another on the couch. Sloppy, impassioned, brute sex.

(*screaming*)

Mommy!!!!!

They fall away from each other in terror and fatigue. Mary clutches wildly at her bathrobe as Henry falls over the coffee table, stumbles to his feet and pulls up his trousers.

Fay is crushed. She breaks out in tears and runs upstairs.

Henry catches his breath and starts after her, but stops, uncertain and confused.

MARY

You bastard!

HENRY

What?

MARY

Get out!

INT. WORLD OF DONUTS – DAY

Simon is asleep with his head down on the table. He wakes finally and sees . . .

Henry sitting across from him, gripping a beer and reading the poem. He finishes, shuts the book and drinks.

> HENRY

Listen. I know a man. He's a big shot in the publishing business. Angus James. Smart, adventurous and tons of integrity. When this thing is ready, I'll recommend he reads it. He'll respect my opinion.

Simon takes this in, then looks down at his hands and proceeds carefully.

> SIMON

A man was here today looking for you.

> HENRY
> (*alert*)

What man?

> SIMON

I don't know. He drove by the house a few times.

Henry throws his eyes heavenward and pulls his hair. Jumping to his feet, he paces maniacally.

> HENRY

Why do they torment me like this? Why? They're like a bunch of fucking mosquitoes!

A customer a few tables away gets nervous and leaves.

> SIMON

What do they want from you?

> HENRY

They want to suffocate me, Simon! They wanna extinguish me like a flame!

Some kid named Tim, sitting at another table, turns around and asks . . .

TIM

But why?

HENRY

They're afraid, that's why! They're afraid of what I might do!
What I might say! Think! They're afraid of my ideas!

He drinks, then returns and sits beside Simon.

You and I are alike in this way, Simon.

SIMON

Yeah?

HENRY

We're outsiders. We think and feel too much and too deeply.
And the world can't handle that. Our mere existence is a
threat to its illusion of security. Sure, they'll name a wing of a
new library after us when we're dead! But now . . . Now,
when we're alive . . . Now, they wanna burn us at the stake!

*He drinks, burps, then slams down the can. He glances over at Tim who
is still looking on.*

Scram.

*Tim hesitates, but then obeys. He gets up and leaves. Henry returns to
Simon.*

For example, I made love to your mother about half an hour
ago and now I'm beginning to think that maybe it wasn't such
a good idea.

Simon blinks. Henry adds . . .

I mean to say, I think Fay may be jealous.

*Simon is deeply confused. He looks ill. He stands and takes a few steps
away, staring at the floor.*

SIMON

I don't want to think about this.

HENRY

Bad move, Simon.

Simon stops and looks at him.

(*pointing at him*)

A poet has got to be able to think about anything.

Simon pauses, then comes closer to Henry and stops.

SIMON

Am I really a poet?

Henry jumps up, strides around the store and speaks at the top of his voice.

HENRY

Of course you are! A great poet! But you need experience. You need to do something to be ashamed of every once in a while, for cryin' out loud.

He walks to the door.

Come on! Let's go out! There's a den of iniquity right across the street! You got any money?

He strides out of the store.

Simon stands there, stunned and looks at Mr Deng as the old man wipes off the table with a wet rag.

INT. THE INFERNO – NIGHT

Later that night.

Henry is dancing wildly on the bar with two sloppy-drunk topless dancers. The place is rocking and the crowd cheers them on.

Simon sits perched on a stool, gripping the bar with white knuckles and clutching a beer, looking on in terror as . . .

Henry starts stripping.

INT. THE GRIM HOUSE – NIGHT

Later that night.

Simon stumbles in and heads upstairs. But he stops, seeing . . .

Mary, sitting on the top step, smoking. She looks guilty and tense. So does Simon.

MARY

That man's a bad influence.

SIMON

On who?

She gets up and storms into her room.

INT. FAY'S ROOM – NIGHT

Moments later.

Simon comes upstairs and stops outside his bedroom door when he sees . . .

Fay, passed out drunk on her bed. Her clothes are half off and her lipstick smeared. She still grips a bottle of tequila in her hand.

Simon hesitates, but then goes in and removes her shoes. He gets her out of her jacket and rolls her into the bed.

Her bare limbs have their effect on Simon and he finds himself staring at her thigh.

He reaches out and almost caresses her leg where her hiked-up skirt reveals the bottom of her behind. He catches himself, snaps his hand away and covers Fay with a blanket.

He flees.

INT. SIMON'S ROOM – NIGHT

Moments later.

Simon is alone in the room with his bed.

The pale sheets beckon.

He is flushed. He blinks.

INT. THE GRIM HOUSE KITCHEN – NIGHT

Moments later.

He creeps down the stairs with an arm-load of books. Sitting at the table, he wrenches a nearby lamp into a more useful position and begins to read.

DISSOLVE TO:

INT. THE GRIM HOUSE – DAY

The next morning.

Henry stumbles up the stoop carrying a laptop computer, its various accessories and a couple of coffees.

He lets himself in and dumps the computer on the kitchen counter.

Simon is asleep on the couch, still in his clothes.

>   HENRY
>   (*shoving him*)
>   Simon. Hey, Simon.
>   (*Simon wakes*)
>   Come on. I got ya some coffee.

Henry trudges back to the kitchen, where he whips out his red pen and immediately begins to correct Simon's poem.

Simon rolls off the couch and makes his way to the table. Seeing the computer . . .

>   SIMON   •
>   What's this?

>   HENRY
>   It's a computer. You write on it.

He reaches into his pocket.

>   Here's the manual.

Simon looks over the computer and flips through the manual.

>   SIMON
>   Where'd you get it?

>   HENRY
>   I stole it. Now listen. Remember how yesterday we discussed

the relative desirability of cadence in relation to the
readability of . . .

> FAY
> (*off*)

Oh, shit! Not you again!

*Fay is on the stairs, hungover and disgusted. Henry throws up his hands
and gets up to go.*

> HENRY

Simon, I can't work under these conditions.

> FAY

Yeah! Get outta here, you freak!

> HENRY

Get a life!

> FAY

Eat shit and die, Henry!

Mary throws open her bedroom door.

> MARY
> (*screaming*)

Beast! Fiend! Rapist!

> FAY

Oh, shut up, Mom!

*Fay stomps back upstairs. Mary slams her door shut. Simon runs out
after Henry.*

EXT. WORLD OF DONUTS – DAY

Moments later.

*Simon follows Henry out into the street and over towards World Of
Donuts . . .*

> SIMON

Henry, wait up!

> HENRY

I am not a rapist!

But Henry stops short, seeing . . .

Officer Buñuel enter World of Donuts.

Shit. Come on, this way.

And he runs down the street in the opposite direction. Simon hangs back, but then follows . . .

INT. CHURCH – DAY

Moments later.

They scramble in and Henry is out of breath. He slumps down into a pew.

> HENRY
> Keep a look out. Tell me when he's gone.

Simon does, but then . . .

> SIMON
> Henry, what's going on? Who is that guy? What's he want?

> HENRY
> He wants to help me! He wants to be my friend.

He pats his pockets, looking for his smokes. Simon looks on, baffled. He comes closer.

> SIMON
> Help you with what?

> HENRY
> (*suddenly*)
> Shhh!

He hears something, stands and moves further into the church. Simon hesitates, but then follows. They hear someone crying. Finally, in a pew off to one side in the shadows, they find . . .

A young priest named Father Hawkes. He's a wreck. He looks up from his quiet sobbing and sees . . .

Henry and Simon standing there looking on with embarrassed distaste. He lowers his head in shame. Henry moves closer and sits beside the distraught priest.

What's wrong?

The priest sighs hopelessly.

FATHER HAWKES

I doubt.

Henry leans back with a sigh and reaches for his cigarettes.

HENRY

So, you're an honest man. Why beat yourself up about it?

He offers a cigarette to the priest and he accepts.

FATHER HAWKES

I don't know if there are grounds for faith. Is my vocation relevant? Does it make a difference?

SIMON

A difference in what?

FATHER HAWKES

The world. The way it is. Is this a way to help relieve suffering?

HENRY

Your vocation makes a difference.

FATHER HAWKES

How can you be so sure?

HENRY

Because vocation *is* the difference. Only someone who really cares doubts. Listen, father, as I was about to tell my friend Simon here, I am, without doubt, the biggest sinner within a hundred miles of this parish. But still, I've gotta stay up late at night to outdo the unending parade of mundane little atrocities I see committed every day right out in the open spaces of this loud and sunlit culture we call home.

FATHER HAWKES

You seem to me to be a sensitive and generous man.

HENRY

I like to think so. But the fact is I appreciate depravity.

Nevertheless, I insist your vocation makes a difference, because to hold out anything other than a spiritual yardstick to reality is to be jerking off grandly into the abyss. Listen, have you got any money? Let's go have a drink.

EXT. WORLD OF DONUTS – DAY

Warren is stopping people on their way in and out of World of Donuts.

> WARREN
> Excuse me, miss, are you a registered voter?

> MISS
> Oh God, really I don't know.

> WARREN
> Well, I'd like to give you some information about Congressman Owen Feer. This man is gunna make a big difference in the lives of every American in the years to come . . .

> MISS
> Thanks, sure. I gotta go, thanks.

A man, Bill, steps up . . .

> WARREN
> Pardon me, sir . . .

> BILL
> Fuck off!

> WARREN
> Right.

Warren stands back and loosens his tie. He looks over at Pearl age seven, who is sitting outside the store.

What time's your mother get off work?

She doesn't respond. He shakes his head and approaches. He sees Fay exit the store . . .

Fay, are you a registered voter?

49

FAY
(*stopping*)
Don't you dare talk that way to me! And keep your hands off
my brother. Pearl, what are you doing here?

WARREN
I'm watchin' her.

Fay figures it out and approaches.

FAY
You and Vicky get back together?

WARREN
I gotta regular job now and everything.

She lifts a flyer and reads.

FAY
I saw this retard on TV this morning.

WARREN
He's gunna be the next president of the United States of
America, Fay.

FAY
Keep dreamin' Warren. The guy's a Nazi.

WARREN
I like him!

FAY
Gimme a light.

WARREN
(*lighting her cigarette*)
He's a decent man. He takes complicated issues and totally
simplifies them. And I appreciate that.

FAY
You still sell dope?

WARREN
No. You know what the problem is with this country, Fay?
Me. I'm the problem. We live in a culture of poverty and

crime, where the work ethic is undermined and male responsibility is made irrelevant.

She studies him a moment more, lost, then shakes her head and helps the child off the car.

> FAY
> Come on, Pearl, let's go play at my house.

> WARREN
> She gives you any trouble, Fay, you just let me know.

INT. THE INFERNO – DAY

An hour later.

Henry and Father Hawkes are drinking. Simon leans on the bar, nodding off to sleep. After a while, Father Hawkes leans back and . . .

> FATHER HAWKES
> Do you think human beings are innately bad?

> HENRY
> Worse than bad! Monstrous! But I love that about them.
> (*banging on the bar*)
> Wake up, Simon!

Simon falls off his bar stool.

EXT. WORLD OF DONUTS – DAY

Moments later.

Warren straightens his tie and looks over to see . . .

Simon stagger up.

Warren shakes his head in dismay and approaches. Simon steadies himself against the wall of the building.

> WARREN
> Jesus Christ, Simon, you're letting yourself go to hell! You read that flyer I gave you?

> SIMON
> What?

> WARREN

Simon, wake up and smell the coffee, huh! It's up to guys like you and me to help create a better tomorrow!

Simon is lost.

INT. WORLD OF DONUTS – DAY

Moments later.

He staggers into World of Donuts and heads for the coffee machine, but stops when he sees Buñuel talking to Mr Deng. Buñuel looks over. Their eyes lock.

EXT. WORLD OF DONUTS – DAY

Same time.

> WARREN
> (*to Vicky*)

Why would I steal a computer from the campaign office?

> VICKY

I'm not saying you did, I'm just saying one *was* and since you *do* have this criminal background . . .

Whack!!! He slaps her . . .

> WARREN
> (*pointing*)

Don't judge me!

Simon runs out of the store and limps away towards home as Buñuel storms out in pursuit. Simon tries to run, but Buñuel catches him easily.

> BUÑUEL

Look, I know you know him. People have seen you around together.

Simon ceases to struggle, but shakes himself free and stands looking down at his feet. Buñuel stands aside and watches him a moment, then reaches in his jacket and brings out his badge.

I'm his parole officer.

Simon studies the badge and waits a little, before asking . . .

> SIMON

What did he do?

> BUÑUEL

I'm not supposed to talk about that stuff with people.

> SIMON

He's my. Friend.

Buñuel pauses, then puts away his badge and looks around the parking lot.

> BUÑUEL

Mr Deng says you're some sort of a poet, or something.

Simon doesn't corroborate this. He looks away and readjusts his sling. Buñuel scratches his head, satisfied and prepares to leave. But first . . .

You tell Henry to call me – Officer Buñuel – pronto! Or they're gunna chuck his ass straight back into jail! Got it?

Simon shrugs.

Buñuel waits a moment, then steps away and gets back in his car. Simon watches as the parole officer drives away and passes . . .

> WARREN

Vicky, look I'm sorry.

> VICKY

Don't you even come near me!

INT. THE GRIM HOUSE KITCHEN – DAY

Later.

> FAY

What do you mean, you quit?

> SIMON

I quit my job.

> FAY

Why!

SIMON

There are things I want to do.

FAY

Like what?

Simon thinks of trying to explain, but then decides not to.

SIMON

'Opportunity will step out of the way to let a man . . . pass it by.'

FAY

Are you drunk?

SIMON

Now you have to go out and get a job!

FAY

I am not gettin' a job!
                              (*paces, then*)
Who's gunna look after Mom!

SIMON

I will.

Fay looks at the ceiling and sighs.

FAY

Pearl, go outside.

They wait as the child goes outside.

Mary listens, unseen, from her bedroom door.

Fay comes over and frowns at her brother. She's about to lecture him, but he cuts her off.

SIMON

If you treat Mom like a sick person, she's gunna stay like . . . you know, a sick person.

Fay tries to control herself. She sighs tiredly and attempts to reason with him . . .

Simon, don't be retarded . . .

SIMON
(*banging the table*)

I am not retarded!

Fay steps back, startled. Simon stands, but can't decide which way to go. He sits back down.

I can see with my own eyes.

Mary turns away from her door and sits on her bed.

Fay leans over the stove, where a large pot of water is beginning to boil.

FAY

Mom can't be left alone with no one to keep an eye on her.

Simon is frustrated and lashes out.

SIMON

Well, who's been keeping an eye on her while you've been out getting fucked by every OTB winner in town?

Fay's mouth falls open and she staggers back, hurt.

Simon regrets it already and stands to leave, scared. But Fay grabs the pot off the stove and hurls it at him, splashing boiling water all over his back.

Aggghhhh!!!

Outside, Pearl turns and looks back at the house.

Simon lies gasping on the floor of the kitchen. Fay falls back against the stove, terrified and drops her head into her hands.

INT. THE GRIM HOUSE BATHROOM – DAY

Later.

Fay is crouched on the floor, sobbing, while Simon lies in a tub of cold water. Mary comes in with a pathetic little freezer tray of ice cubes and dumps them into the tub.

She steps back into the hall and throws the ice tray down the stairs. She glares back at Fay, who cries even louder as Simon stares up at the ceiling.

Mary shakes her head and walks into her room, slamming the door behind her.

> FAY
> (*sniffling*)
> What happened to her, Simon? How did she get this way? Will it happen to me too? Huh? Why are we so fucked up?

Simon has no answers. But he reaches out and touches his sister's hand.

INT. LIBRARY – DAY

Evening.

Simon comes limping in, all stiff because of his scalded back. He's not familiar with the library, so he stands looking around, trying to figure it out.

INT. LIBRARY STACKS – DAY

Moments later.

He wanders into an aisle, overwhelmed by all the books. Coming to the far end of the aisle, he looks off to his left and sees Henry sitting on a small stool, reading, with ten or twenty open volumes scattered around him on the floor.

> SIMON
> (*approaching*)
> Henry?

> HENRY
> (*looking up and rising*)
> Simon! What are you doing here?

> SIMON
> Henry . . . Your parole officer, Officer Buñuel, came by again today.

Henry sighs and sits back down.

He told me to tell you that if you don't call him they're gunna put you back in jail.

>   HENRY

Simon . . .

>   SIMON

He gave me this number . . .

>   HENRY

Simon . . .

>   SIMON

He was talking to Mr Deng too, and, well, you know, I was thinking . . .

>   HENRY

Simon, just shut the fuck up!

Simon blinks and looks down at his feet, unable to respond. Deeply hurt, he simply turns to walk away. But Henry reaches out and grabs his arm. Simon stops, pauses and looks back at his friend.

Forgive me.

He lets go and turns away on his stool.

Forgive me, Simon.

Simon comes back over to him.

>   SIMON

Call him, Henry. Please.

Henry gives in slowly to the inevitable. He sighs deeply and stands, handing Simon a book . . .

>   HENRY

OK. Look, do me a favor. You got a library card?

>   SIMON

Yeah.

>   HENRY

Check this out for me.

Simon looks at the cover: Paradise Lost.

> **HENRY**
> Milton. Seventeenth century. English. You see, Simon, it's important my 'Confession' dig up the past, comb previous evidence and help chart the historic – even the aesthetic – inevitability of my ideas. And . . .

A young woman passes by, scanning the stacks. She and Henry have a split second of eye contact, then she turns and moves away. Henry straightens his tie and watches her go.

> This place is crawling with chicks, Simon. Wander around. Leer a little. Cop a feel. Impose yourself on 'em. See what happens.

> **SIMON**
> I make girls uncomfortable.

> **HENRY**
> Bullshit! You've got a rough hewn charm that sets 'em on edge. Now, listen, I gotta go.

> **SIMON**
> Henry?

Henry stops and turns. Simon pauses, then . . .

> What did you do?

Henry watches him for a moment, then swaggers closer . . .

> **HENRY**
> I got caught.

Simon waits for more but is disappointed. With one final cracked grin at his friend, Henry throws back his shoulders, slicks back his hair and strides off. Simon watches him go and frowns, not comforted. He flips through the pages of Paradise Lost.

> **SIMON**
> (*voice over*)
> 'Whereto with speedy words the arch-fiend replied
> Fallen Cherub, to be weak is miserable . . .'

INT. LIBRARY READING ROOM – DAY

Moments later.

He comes out from the stacks, working his way through the first page of Paradise Lost. *He nearly bumps into a girl and they stop and look at one another. He tries to hold her gaze for a moment, challenging himself, but then turns away and stalks to a table. He sits and leans over the page.*

After a moment, though, he lifts his face and glances at . . .

Another girl, sitting further down the table. She looks up from her reading and returns his gaze.

He smiles at her.

She gets up and leaves.

Simon frowns, confounded and returns to his book. He takes out his notebook and pencil, meaning to take notes, but sees instead . . .

A third girl sitting at another table, listening to her Walkman and typing her homework into a laptop computer.

He finds himself staring at her and forces himself back to his book. But he can't help himself and glances back over at her.

With a sigh, he begins to write in his notebook . . .

> SIMON
> (*voice-over*)
> Why is it this beautiful girl makes me sad? Does she know how beautiful she is? Do people tell her? Does she ever feel stupid?

He looks back over at her. She happens to look up and their eyes meet. She smiles. Horrified, he looks down.

> Why don't I smile when she looks at me? I look away. Ashamed of myself.

He watches her again, thinks, then writes . . .

> Her figure makes me violent. I want to somehow break her. But tenderly. How is this possible? Ask Henry.

He writes a few moments more, scribbling across the page, then stops and looks back over at the girl.

(*voice-over*)

I can't breathe.

He tears out the page and folds it in half. Then he gets up and crosses the room to where the girl is busily engaged in her work. She looks up, sees him, and removes her headset with a pleasant smile. He places his note on the table before her, then turns and walks quickly away.

The girl watches him go, confused, then lifts the note and reads . . .

(*voice-over*)

Why do I do this to myself? And why do I reduce you to only one possibility? These are not even questions anymore. I know the answers myself. This isn't a page of notes. It's a letter. A letter to you. A desperate act. You are a miracle to me. I can't breathe.

By now, Simon is gone from the library. The girl finishes reading the letter and looks around in astonishment.

INT. WORLD OF DONUTS – DAY

Evening.

Henry enters and sits with Buñuel.

                              BUÑUEL
How are you, Henry?

                              HENRY
                            (*frowning*)
Peachy. Gimme a light.

                              BUÑUEL
Have you found a job?

Henry just glares at him and smokes.

How 'bout those Alcoholics Anonymous meetings, did you go over and visit them yet?

HENRY

What happened to this assistant librarian position you were
supposed to set me up with?

Buñuel looks down, disappointed.

BUÑUEL

I tried, Henry. I really did.

HENRY

So what happened?

BUÑUEL

Henry, with your background . . . Well, I mean, with your
record, they didn't think it'd be right to have you at the
neighborhood library.

HENRY

Why not?

BUÑUEL

They thought you'd be a bad influence on the kids.

Henry sits back, offended.

(*adds*)

Or worse.

HENRY

So my word is not enough. My promise worthless. The fact
I've served my time nothing but the emblem of my
continuing guilt.

BUÑUEL

Apparently.

Henry leans back and sighs, furious and indignant.

INT. THE GRIM HOUSE – NIGHT

*Simon comes in, excited and preoccupied, and finds Fay working at the
computer.*

FAY

What's up?

(*guiltily*)

Nothing.

FAY

I'm creating my résumé. This computer's got a program
especially for it. I bought some special stationery too. It's
scented. Look.

*She shoves a sheath of papers up under his nose and he backs away in
disgust.*

It's roses.

Simon takes his notebooks from a cabinet above the fridge.

SIMON

Can you type my poem into that thing?

FAY
(*shocked*)

That's your poem?

SIMON

Yeah.

FAY
(*smokes, then*)

Simon, Mom's right about you. A poem's supposed to be a
small, delicate kinda thing. Kinda feminine. Gentle. Look at
this. You've made a fuckin' telephone book.

*He places the notebooks on the table and leaves the house. Fay clears the
computer screen, pulls the notebooks closer and gets down to work.*

INT. HENRY'S APARTMENT – NIGHT

Moments later.

*Simon arrives with a six-pack and finds Henry sitting in front of the
fire, staring into the flames, brooding darkly.*

HENRY

I was caught. Yes, I was caught . . . once. I was caught *in
flagranti delicto* screwing a thirteen-year-old girl named Susan.

She was an ugly and mean-spirited kid, but she knew how to play upon my weaknesses which, I admit, are deep and many.

He drinks, then looks at Simon and adds . . .

You appear shocked.

SIMON
(he is)

Sorry.

Henry stands and leans over the fire.

HENRY

It was a pathetic little conspiracy. A transparently desperate attempt to discredit me and my ideas; to label me a mere pedophile. As if I'd be ashamed of such a thing. As if Socrates himself hadn't been taken out of circulation for corrupting the youth of Athens!

He comes over and takes a beer. He strides around the room, thinking, reflecting.

Seven years. Seven years for one afternoon of blissful transgression. But what of it? Who cares? Prison's not so bad; particularly if one's a sex offender, free from the popular and conventional horror of sodomy.

Stops, drinks declares . . .

They were not 'lost years'.

He approaches the notebooks lined up on the mantelpiece.

I put them to good use. I began my major work. My opus.

He glances over at Simon, who sits gripping his beer, watching, rapt.

Believe me, Simon, this incident with the girl, prison . . . It pales to insignificance in the wider context of my career.

He pauses and swills back some beer. He brightens up, gets excited . . .

Nothing in comparison to the day my 'Confession' is unleashed.

> *(beginning to pace)*
>
> What an orgy we'll have then, huh? What shouts of outrage from the offended populace, from the sanctimonious purveyors of culture and quality, the righteous defenders of what ever inane and haphazard notion of progress then in vogue. They'll be beside themselves with fiercely reasoned critical analysis. Apoplectic with indignation!

Drinks sloppily, burps, wipes his mouth with his arm.

> Their feelings will be hurt.

He smashes the bottle in the fireplace.

> Yes, like a mirror which reflects only the inside of the person before it, my 'Confession' will lovingly render humanity's common monstrosity in all of its lurid wide screen glory.

He grabs a new beer and twists off its cap.

> Why should I blush or feel shame before the common lot of humanity, anyway, for a few banal and, again I admit, inelegant transgressions?

He drinks, sighs and sits back down.

> After all, really, I'm doing civilization a favor.

Simon sits back in awe. He waits a moment and thinks. Finally he stands and approaches the 'Confession'. He reaches out and drags his hand across the notebooks.

SIMON
When can I read it?

Henry sits staring into the flames again. He pauses, then . . .

HENRY
Soon.

INT. CHURCH – DAY

Next day.

Simon and Father Hawkes are deep in conversation.

64

FATHER HAWKES

We are told not to judge. But to forgive. Not to look into our neighbor's eye to find the bad, but to find the good.

(*pacing*)

Now this is difficult. I admit.

(*pause*)

But having a good friend is not always easy.

Simon listens and carefully considers all the priest says.

SIMON

Yes, but . . . do you think Henry is . . . dangerous?

Father Hawkes pauses, then comes closer and sits.

FATHER HAWKES

He needs help. Our help. Yours especially.

SIMON

But what can I do?

FATHER HAWKES

The best parts of himself come to the surface when he's helping someone learn. I've seen this. Let yourself be taught. Show your appreciation for his guidance. In this way, you know, perhaps. Well. There's hope for everyone. Even. Even Henry.

INT. WORLD OF DONUTS – DAY

Fay comes walking up through the parking lot with Simon's notebooks and a pile of typed papers. She's a wreck; tear-stained face and a ball of tissues gripped in her hand like a weapon. She throws open the door to the World of Donuts and looks around.

The place is crowded with teenagers hanging around like it was a café or student union.

Fay sniffles tragically and falls on the counter.

FAY

Gnoc, gimme a value pack of Kleenex, will ya?

Gnoc gets the Kleenex while Fay overhears two kids near Simon's poem . . .

TIM

The violence of the imagery reminds me of early Clash, while the lyricism of the verse recalls, for me, Walt Whitman.

BIBI

I would have said Dickinson, maybe even Eliot, and so on. But I agree with the punk roots . . .

Fay pays for her tissues and makes her way to the back of the store where she finds Simon with Henry, who is holding forth to his friend and the small coterie of high school students surrounding them . . .

HENRY

The greats all say the same thing: little. And what little there is to be said is immense. Or, in other words, follow your own genius to where it leads without regard for the apparent needs of the world at large, which, in fact, has no needs as such, but, rather, moments of exhaustion in which it is incapable of prejudice.

(*drinks*)

We can only hope to collide with these moments of unselfconsciousness. This divine fatigue . . . this . . .

FAY

(*sitting*)

Push over.

Henry takes the typed manuscript from her and continues . . .

HENRY

As I tried to make plain in Paris: 'Nous savons que nous avons chuté parce que nous savons qui nous sommes.' 'We know we have fallen because we know who we are.'

FAY

(*skeptically*)

When were you in Paris?

HENRY

(*interrupted*)

That's beside the point. But did they listen to me? Of course not!

66

Fay blows her nose and Simon is concerned.

SIMON

You alright, Fay?

FAY
(*lighting a cigarette*)
No, I'm not alright! Your poem brought my period on a week and half early! So just shut up. Everybody just shut up!

She drops her head to the table and cries. Henry and Simon look on in silence. Then Henry continues . . .

HENRY

For is this not the best of all possible worlds? Are not the evils of this world necessary components of a cosmos that could not exist without them?

Amy's girlfriend, Chris, leans forward studiously and asks . . .

CHRIS

So, do you believe in God?

HENRY
(*smokes, shrugs*)
Unfortunately.

FAY
(*lifting her head*)
Yeah, but when were you in Paris?

HENRY
(*aggravated*)
At. One. Time.

CHRIS

Simon, can I have your autograph?

Simon looks from her to Henry. Henry winks at him.

HENRY

Go ahead. But never let yourself be flattered.

Simon signs the girl's book.

FAY
(*to Henry*)
So what about this friend of yours, Hot Shot? The publisher.

HENRY
Who?

SIMON
(*reminding him*)
Angus James.

FAY
Yeah. Angus James. How about sending this poem to him?

Henry seems a bit put upon.

HENRY
Because it's not done yet.

FAY
(*to Simon*)
When's it gunna be done, Simon?

SIMON
I don't know.

FAY
Well, you oughta be home writing instead of hanging out over here with all your groupies.

AMY
Hey, I'm not a groupie.

FAY
Pardon me, swivel-hips. Is that your PowerBook?

AMY
Yeah.

FAY
Can I see it?

Fay and Amy talk tech as . . .

HENRY
(*continues*)
The thing to do is to send parts of it to different magazines
and literary journals first. That kinda thing. You know.
Substantiate it.

AMY
(*looking up*)
What's 'scatalogical' mean?

Henry sips his beer and looks at her.

HENRY
Filth, child. A preoccupation with excrement. Why?

AMY
That's what the Board of Education called Simon's poem,
yesterday; scatological.

Henry reaches across the table and shakes Simon's hand.

INT. THE GRIM HOUSE KITCHEN – DAY

The next day.

Fay is frying something on the stove, a cigarette hangs from her lip. A middle-aged woman with a press ID on her lapel appears at the kitchen door and taps.

> EDNA

Hello?

> FAY

Yeah, I'm listening.

> EDNA

My name is Edna Rodriguez and I write the human interest column for the *Queens County Examiner* and I was just wondering if I could have a word with Simon Grim?

Intrigued, Fay steps over to the door with her spatula. She looks Edna over, studies her ID, then steps away and screams upstairs.

> FAY

Simon!

> EDNA
> (*startled*)

Thank you.

Fay comes back over near the door, waving her spatula.

> FAY

You can't talk to him for, you know, too long or anything, 'cause he's gotta, you know . . . he writes all day. That's all he does. Can you believe that?

No response.

> (*calling again*)

Hey! Simon! Get down here!

Simon finally shuffles into the kitchen.

Simon, this is Edna. She's from the newspaper.

> EDNA
> (*rapid fire*)

Simon, the Parents' Association at the local high school are calling your poem pornography. The teachers are defending the students' right to exercise their critical tastes and sensibilities. The county agrees with the Church and considers the poem emblematic of modern society's moral disintegration. How do you feel about these controversial reactions to your poem?

Simon says nothing. He just stares at her.

FAY
(*punching him*)
Simon, answer the woman.

Simon just looks away, thinks, then wanders back upstairs. Mary passes him on his way out of the kitchen and comes up to Fay and Edna at the door.

MARY
I need my prescription filled.

FAY
Mom, this is Edna. Edna, Mom.

EDNA
Mrs Grim, what was Simon like as a child?

MARY
We all thought he was retarded.

FAY
Everyone did.

MARY
Never said a word.

FAY
He masturbated constantly.

MARY
Had no friends.

FAY
Till he met Henry.

MARY
And that's when all the trouble really started.

INT. HENRY'S APARTMENT – DAY

Henry is shaving. Simon sits in the kitchen, sorting through rejection letters . . .

> SIMON
> (*reading*)
> Dear Mr Grim, we here at the magazine consider ourselves and the publication open-minded and cutting edge and have consistently printed the work of the most brilliant and far-seeing young talent of the day. Every week we are forced to return writing which we can not for one reason or another publish and include a brief but polite refusal. But this tract you've sent us demands a response as violent as the effect your words have had upon us. Drop dead. Keep your day job. Sincerely, The Editors.

> HENRY
> *De gustibus non disputandum est.*

> SIMON
> (*thinking*)
> You can't argue with taste?

> HENRY
> *About* taste. You can't argue about taste. God, Simon.

Simon gives up and pushes the letters away, beaten.

> SIMON
> The other twenty-five are almost as bad. I don't know why I bother.

Henry drops his razor and stomps out into the hall.

> HENRY
> What do you mean you don't know why you bother? You bother because you know the poem is excellent!

> SIMON
> Do I?

> HENRY
> Of course you do!

SIMON

I'm not so sure sometimes.

HENRY

Can you sit there, look me straight in the eye, and tell me you
don't think this poem is great? That it is not at once a work of
great lyrical beauty and ethical depth? That it is not a
genuine, highly individual, and profound meditation on the
miracle of existence?

Simon holds the stare, overwhelmed.

SIMON

I, ah . . .

HENRY

Can you?

Simon looks away, thinks a moment, then looks back at Henry.

SIMON

No. I can't.

HENRY

So, you see, you have no choice!

He goes back into the bathroom. Simon thinks a while, then . . .

SIMON
(*calling*)

Can you recommend it to your friend, the publisher?

No response.

Henry? Can you recommend the poem to him?

*Still no response. Simon gets up and stands in the bathroom doorway.
Henry is shaving.*

I mean, I think it's finished and, for better or worse, it is book
length.

HENRY

That might not be as easy as it seems.

SIMON

Why?

HENRY

Well, it's been a long time. My name might not carry as much
weight as it once did with Angus.

SIMON

But he's your friend, right?

HENRY

We were close at one time.

SIMON

You said he respected your opinion.

Henry puts down his razor and looks at Simon in the mirror.

HENRY

Look, Simon, opinions come and go.

He sees Simon looks worried.

To be honest; my ideas, my writing, they haven't always been
received well or even calmly. They're upsetting. I'm a
controversial man.

He walks around the bathroom, gesticulating.

You see, what I'm doing is too radical. Too uncompromising.
It'll take time for people to see its value. It's ahead of its time,
perhaps, or maybe just . . .
                    (*stops*)
A recommendation from me might do you as much harm as it
does good.

*Simon patiently absorbs all this, then walks through the kitchen and
looks across at the 'Confession' notebooks.*

SIMON

Henry, why can't I read the 'Confession'?

HENRY

Because certain work needs to be experienced all at once in
order for one to appreciate the full force of its character.

INT. WORLD OF DONUTS – DAY

Simon talks with Fay as she eats her lunch.

> FAY
> Simon, wake up! The guy's in a dream world!

> SIMON
> He's afraid that his reputation will prevent people from giving my work an honest chance.

> FAY
> His reputation as what?

> SIMON
> As a writer.

> FAY
> Gimme a break.

> SIMON
> He's kinda like in exile. Marginalized on account of his ideas.

> FAY
> If he's such a great big fat genius, why doesn't he write books? Like you do.

75

SIMON

He has. He's written a book. It's almost completed. He's been working on it for years. It's just not published.

FAY

Yeah, I bet. It's probably disgusting.

SIMON
(*defensively*)
It's a quite serious and difficult piece of work, apparently.

FAY

Have you read it?

SIMON

No. Not yet. Soon. Certain work needs to be experienced all at once in order for one to appreciate the full force of its character.

FAY

Yeah, well, what ever. Listen, Simon, forget Henry. Go straight up to this Angus James character yourself and make him read your poem.

She gets up to go. She's wearing a smart outfit.

I'm gunna apply for a job at the one-hour photo joint and then go over to the Mall to see about that job in the bank. Make sure Mom takes her pills. See ya.

INT. THE GRIM HOUSE – DAY

Mary is sitting, brooding in front of the TV, which displays only static white noise. She turns it off with the remote and sits in silence for a moment.

She gets off the couch and moves to the kitchen table, where Fay's computer sits. She goes over and reaches up above the fridge, opening the cabinet containing Simon's notebooks.

She hesitates, then takes them down and holds them in her hands, as if to begin reading. But then she puts them back.

She walks over to the piano and stands there, hesitating, before slowly

*sitting down and opening it. She lifts her hands to play, then pauses and
looks around behind her, making sure no one is there.*

But, finally, she turns back and begins playing.

*She plays a sad-sounding modern classical piece with rusty
accomplishment. At one time she was probably quite good.*

*She plays for a while, gradually letting herself become moved by the
music. But then she stops, pauses, and looks behind her.*

*Simon is standing in the kitchen. He has been deeply affected by her
playing.*

SIMON

Please don't stop.

*She stares him down a moment longer, then looks away and closes the
piano. She returns to the couch and switches on the TV.*

Simon comes closer. He sits.

That was nice what you were playing.

MARY

Yes, it was nice. But it was unremarkable.

Simon waits. Eventually . . .

Does that matter?

MARY
(*looking right at him*)
Yes. It does.

She gets up off the couch and goes upstairs. She slams her bedroom door and leaves Simon alone on the couch. He thinks. Then, he gets up and goes into the kitchen.

He takes the typed manuscript of his poem from the cabinet above the refrigerator and goes to the door. He pauses, clutches the poem and goes out.

EXT. SUBWAY STATION – DAY

Simon waits, clutching his poem to his side, as a train pulls into the station. Excited and determined, he gets on.

INT. TRAIN – DAY

Simon travels to New York City. He finds an envelope on the floor to put the poem in.

INT. MARY'S ROOM – DAY

Mary wakes up and sits on the edge of the bed, feeling regretful about her tone of voice with Simon.

INT. THE GRIM HOUSE KITCHEN – DAY

Moments later.

Mary comes down into the kitchen and listens.

MARY
Simon?

No answer. She steps over to the cabinet and almost takes down Simon's notebook. But doesn't. She grabs her pills and is about to take them. But then she stops. She puts them down and goes to the cabinet. She takes down Simon's notebooks and sits at the table, pauses, then pulls them closer and begins to read.

INT. PUBLISHING HOUSE LOBBY – DAY

Simon enters a big, posh lobby and checks the registry.

INT. PUBLISHING HOUSE RECEPTION – DAY

Moments later.

Simon comes out of the elevator and enters the reception area of James Midriff and Sutton Publishing. He walks hesitantly up to the receptionist, a bright and spirited young woman named Laura.

> LAURA

Hi, I'll take that.

Simon steps back defensively.

Aren't you the messenger?

> SIMON

No.

> LAURA

Are you here to fix the plumbing?

79

SIMON

I'm here to see Mr Angus James.

LAURA
(*amused*)

Are you?

SIMON

I'm not a plumber. Or a messenger. I was once a garbage man. But now I'm a poet.

Laura steps back, cocks her head and removes her designer eye-wear.

INT. CONFERENCE ROOM – DAY

Same time.

Angus is at a big table with two other men, Steve and Barry.

BARRY

The book, as we know it, Angus, will be a thing of the past within the next few years. Novels, articles, newspapers will all be downloaded on to our personal computers anyway.

ANGUS

So you're telling me to get out of the publishing business?

STEVE

No. But we've got to re-invent the publishing business for the electronic age.

Laura knocks.

ANGUS

Yes, Laura?

LAURA

I'm sorry to disturb you, gentlemen, but . . . Angus, there's a particularly wound-up young garbage man out here who seems to have written a poem. A long poem. And I recall how, at last month's meeting, you stressed the need for us to be on the look-out for more marginalized verse from unestablished quarters of the American scene.

ANGUS

Did I say that?

Steve and Barry nod.

STEVE

Yeah. You did.

BARRY

Twice.

ANGUS

Well, OK. Make an appointment, Laura. Sometime next month.

LAURA

Right-e-o.

And she's gone.

ANGUS
(*returning*)

So, anyway, how is the digital revolution going to help me sell books?

INT. PUBLISHING HOUSE RECEPTION – DAY

Simon looks disappointed.

SIMON

Why can't I see him now?

LAURA
(*sincerely*)

Because he's a very important man and, well, you're not.

Simon just looks down at his shoes. Laura touches his arm and reassures him.

Be reasonable.

He looks up, pauses, then . . .

SIMON

Why?

INT. CONFERENCE ROOM – DAY

Same time.

ANGUS

I don't think people are going to prefer reading books on
television, Steve.

STEVE

It won't be television!

BARRY

It'll be interactive.

STEVE

Angus, look, we have a number of charts here . . .

BARRY

In every home in America the PC will be where the TV used
to be.

STEVE

And it'll be a direct connection to all forms of media.

BARRY

An unprecedented transformation of American social life . . .

STEVE

We'll all become better informed, more literate, increasingly
productive, and . . . Well, and, like I said, we have a number
of charts . . .

Laura re-enters . . .

LAURA

Sorry to disturb you again, gentlemen, but . . . Angus, I'd like
to call security for this one. Though, before I do, I just
wanted to ask just how marginal the as yet undiscovered voice
of American poetry should be?

ANGUS
(*thinking*)
Pretty damn marginal, I'd think.

BARRY

Down right controversial, probably.

ANGUS

How's he strike you?

LAURA

He's been denounced by his local Board of Education.

BARRY

Oh, I read about him in the paper. Hangs out in a delicatessen somewhere and writes pornography.

INT. PUBLISHING HOUSE RECEPTION – DAY

Moments later.

Angus comes out to the water cooler and glares at Simon as he gets a drink.

ANGUS

Hello, and why do you think I should take valuable time out of my busy schedule to read . . .

He grabs the envelope and sees no title.

This?

Simon is stumped. He looks over at Laura, who purses her lips and tilts her head. He twists a button on his shirt, thinking, then returns to Angus.

SIMON

Because it's a masterpiece.

ANGUS

Really?

SIMON

Yes.

ANGUS
(*to Laura*)

Are you hearing this?

LAURA

He's adorable.

SIMON

I wouldn't want to waste your time.

ANGUS

I'm sure you wouldn't and I appreciate you being so straightforward.

SIMON

Thank you.

ANGUS

I assume you can take straightforward criticism?

Simon looks over at Laura.

LAURA

Just say 'Yes'.

SIMON
(*looking back*)

Maybe.

ANGUS

Get him a coffee, Laura.

LAURA

Have a seat, Mr Grim.

ANGUS

Hold my calls for the next half hour.

LAURA

What about Steve?

ANGUS

He doesn't drink coffee. Steve, do you drink coffee?

STEVE
(*off*)

Angus, listen to me!

INT. WORLD OF DONUTS – DAY

Henry paces back and forth. With the fingers of one hand pressed against his forehead and his eyes closed tight in concentration, he dictates to Amy, who is sitting at a table with her laptop computer, typing his every word.

> HENRY
> In the infinite amplitude of his love, God wants to create the largest number of best elements that can exist together in one cosmos . . . OK.

Amy types away, fascinated by Henry's intelligence.

> In an instantaneous calculation made in eternity, God computes the best possible world and creates it. Fine. This 'decision' by God is uncontingent and eternal rather than temporally or ontologically sequential.

Stops, zeroing in on his point.

> AMY
> How do you spell that?

> HENRY
> What?

> AMY
> Ontologically.

> HENRY
> O-N-T . . . Don't you have some kinda spell-check on that thing?

> AMY
> Never mind.

> HENRY
> It is impossible for every perfect good to be compatible with every other perfect good. The intense beauty of the mountain must be set off by the fertility of the plain, so to speak.

He smokes, drinks, paces some more. Amy waits with bated breath, devastated by his obscure profundity. He comes back and sits beside her, reaching his conclusion.

The good of freewill must entail real choices for sin.

She gazes at his profile, in love.

Henry sits thinking and Amy watches him reverently. She leans over close and whispers in his ear. He turns and looks at her, alarmed.

HENRY

Listen, Amy, back off. I'm on parole.

AMY

You feel the same way. I can tell. I can see it when you look at me.

Henry jumps up and looks around, paranoid. He keeps his voice down and points at her.

HENRY

Hey! I don't look at you.

AMY

Yes you do. In the street. In the parking lot yesterday. That night on the highway.

HENRY

I look at a lot of people that way.

Disappointed, Amy turns away and sulks.

AMY

You think I'm stupid.

Henry sees she's genuinely upset and feels bad. He sits back down and lays his hand on hers.

HENRY

No, as a matter of fact, I think you're a real bright kid and I like that about you.

AMY
(*looks up, pouts*)

You do?

Now Henry tries to scare her away. He leers at her.

HENRY

I like it so much I've got half a mind to do perverse things to you. Right here. Right now. Things you might just learn to like.

She just stares at him, blinks, then looks away and tries to imagine this. She takes her laptop and leaves, confused and blushing.

Henry watches her go and grins, satisfied with himself.

INT. PUBLISHING HOUSE RECEPTION – DAY

Angus throws on his coat and thrusts the poem at Simon as they walk down the hall.

ANGUS

This is really quite unbelievably bad, my friend. I mean, I'm all for experimentation and I've made a career out of a healthy disregard for convention, but . . . Look, this is profoundly irrelevant material. This is only my opinion. But it's an opinion I value highly. Goodnight, Laura. Call Norton Press. We're still on for tomorrow.

Simon looks pale as Angus strides towards the elevator.

I've been wrong before as a publisher. But I refuse to admit I've ever been wrong as a reader. You have talent, I admit. You have an innate sense of the musicality of language. A good ear, maybe. But you do nothing significant with it. And this twisted reasoning that poses as . . . conviction or insight, it's . . . well, it's embarrassing.

They reach the elevator and stop. Simon tries to catch his breath.

Why did you bring this thing to me, anyway?

SIMON
(*weakly*)
A friend of mine spoke of you. He said you had a lot of integrity.

ANGUS

Yes, well, of course, I do. But I'm not crazy, am I? Who is this person? Do I know him?

Simon hesitates, almost decides against it, but then . . .

                         SIMON
      Henry Fool.

Angus looks back at him.

Simon waits.

Angus looks aside, thinks, then shakes his head.

                         ANGUS
      Never heard of him.

Simon just looks at him blankly, confused.

The doors slide open and Angus gets in the elevator. He's gone. Simon sinks into a chair and stares at the carpet. He is so surprised and hurt he gasps for breath.

His poem slips from his hand and falls to the floor.

                         LAURA
                         (off)
      I remember Henry.

Simon doesn't register this right away. But then he looks up and over at the receptionist.

Laura stands and comes around her desk. She pauses, seeing his disappointment, then comes closer and picks up his poem. Handing it to him, she explains . . .

      He used to be the janitor here.

He just stares at her, demolished.

EXT. SIDEWALK/SUBWAY ENTRANCE – DAY

Later.

Simon dumps his poem in a trash can, pauses, then enters the subway.

INT. WORLD OF DONUTS – DAY

Henry is leaning on the counter, flipping through pornographic magazines and smoking.

MR DENG
(*off*)
Henry, put those magazines back.

HENRY
I'm just looking at the pictures.

MR DENG
It's not good for you.

Henry flips through pages and nods, impressed.

HENRY
I learn so much from these magazines, Mr Deng. I refuse to discriminate between modes of knowing.

MR DENG
And you can't smoke in here anymore.

Henry looks up, outraged.

HENRY
Why not!

MR DENG
It's the law.

Henry throws his cigarette to the floor, steps on it and returns to his magazine.

HENRY
This place is losing all its charm, Mr Deng.

MR DENG
Business is good. The kids, they hang out all day and drink coffee, talk about art and read poetry.

Henry shakes his head in dismay and studies a centerfold.

HENRY
It's just a fad, Mr Deng. These kids today, they're just slaves to fashion.

INT. THE GRIM HOUSE KITCHEN – DAY

Same time.

Fay comes in, hot and tired from walking around in high heels.

> ### FAY
> Anybody home? Mom?

She stands on the stairs and hears the water running in the bathroom.

> Ma, that you?

No answer. She discovers she's out of cigarettes.

INT. WORLD OF DONUTS – DAY

Henry is leaning on the counter with a six-pack of beer, pleading with Mr Deng.

> ### HENRY
> Come on, Mr Deng! How much do I owe you?

> ### MR DENG
> Twenty-five dollars.

> ### HENRY
> That can't be right! And so what? My credit's good.

Warren comes in.

> ### WARREN
> Henry!

> ### HENRY
> Hey, Warren, you gotta couple of bucks I can borrow?

Warren reaches for his wallet.

> ### WARREN
> Listen, Henry, I wanna remind you to vote this Thursday.

> ### HENRY
> Ah, yes, of course. When noble minds shrink from the task of leadership scoundrels will rush in to fill the void.
> > (*takes cash*)
> Thanks.

> ### WARREN
> It's every American's right. A blessing. Yet another opportunity to save America from itself.

Henry pays Mr Deng for his beer.

INT. HENRY'S APARTMENT – DAY

Moments later.

Fay bangs on the door.

> FAY
> Hey, Henry, you in there? Gimme a cigarette.

No answer. She tries the door. It's open. She hesitates.

> Henry?

She goes quietly in.

EXT. WORLD OF DONUTS – DAY

Moments later.

Henry steps out of the store and stops when he sees Amy standing there, pouting. He looks away and sighs. Amy picks at the fabric of her stockings and bites her lip.

> AMY
> Henry?

Henry smokes.

> HENRY
> Yeah.

> AMY
> What kind of . . . Well, I mean . . . What kind of . . . perverse things would you do to me?

It's more than he can stand. He holds his head.

> HENRY
> Take a powder, cupcake.

> AMY
> No, really.

Evaporate!

Crushed, she breaks out in tears and flees.

INT. THE GRIM HOUSE – DAY

Same time.

Simon comes in, furious and throws open the fridge. He finds nothing to eat or drink. He slams the door, then hears the water running in the bathroom upstairs. He stops and listens.

The bathroom door; the water heard running steadily.

Simon turns away then sees . . .

The poem notebooks face down on the table.

He thinks.

The bathroom door; the water heard running . . .

INT. HENRY'S APARTMENT – DAY

Moments later.

Henry comes into his house, hot and bothered, cradling his six-pack. But he stops, listens, then steps through the kitchen towards the living-room. He stops in the entrance and sees . . .

Fay on the floor of the living-room, reading his 'Confession', her mouth hung open in an astonished 'O'.

He drops his six-pack and . . .

She spins around, caught in the act.

Henry stands in the doorway, pent up, sweating and with perverse things on his mind.

Fay, her hands palm down on the floor behind her, bites her lip, coquettishly.

Henry looks her over like she was something good to eat.

She feels his gaze all over her and twists to one side with a breathless little shudder.

He steps nearer, stands over her and she looks up at him.

INT. THE GRIM HOUSE – DAY

Same time.

Simon climbs the stairs to the bathroom . . .

INT. HENRY'S APARTMENT – DAY

Same time.

Henry and Fay kissing passionately . . .

INT. THE GRIM HOUSE – DAY

Same time.

Simon knocks on the bathroom door.

INT. HENRY'S APARTMENT – DAY

Same time.

Henry and Fay groping and shoving one another as they stagger from room to room.

INT. THE GRIM HOUSE – DAY

Same time.

Simon bangs on the bathroom door.

INT. HENRY'S APARTMENT – DAY

Same time.

Fay falls to the couch . . .

INT. THE GRIM HOUSE – DAY

Same time.

Simon crashes through the door and finds . . .

Mary, kneeling over the edge of the tub, her wrists slit and the blood running down the drain, the shower raining down over her back.

Simon looks on in horror.

INT. HENRY'S APARTMENT – DAY

Same time.

Henry tears open his trousers . . .

INT. THE GRIM HOUSE – DAY

Same time.

Simon lifts Mary from the bathtub.

INT. HENRY'S APARTMENT – DAY

Same time.

Henry and Fay clutch and grind and heave . . .

INT. THE GRIM HOUSE – DAY

Same time.

Simon drags his mother from the bathroom and down the stairs.

94

INT. HENRY'S APARTMENT – DAY

Same time.

Henry and Fay are making mad, passionate love, oblivious to the world around them.

INT. GRIM HOUSE DAY – DAY

Same time.

Simon drags Mary through the house.

INT. HENRY'S APARTMENT – DAY

Same time.

Henry and Fay fuck.

EXT. THE GRIM HOUSE – DAY

Same time.

Simon drags Mary out the kitchen door and into the yard, looking desperately for help. He reaches the street, her limp body hanging grotesquely before him, and looks helplessly up and down the block.

DISSOLVE TO:

EXT. CEMETERY – DAY

Simon, Henry, Mr Deng, Fay, Gnoc and Buñuel stand with Father Hawkes at the grave.

FATHER HAWKES
Let us pray. Lord, grant that peace be within reach for our friend, Mary. May the pain and confusion she endured on earth be fought through in the after life, so that she may enter the Kingdom of Heaven and live in the light of God. Amen.

He sprinkles holy water on the coffin and they all drop carnations at the grave. Simon and Fay remain there looking down at the coffin. Henry waits for them a few yards away, wishing he could help, but feeling out of place.

95

EXT. JUNKYARD – DAY

Simon is back working on the garbage truck. He collects garbage and throws it in the truck as Henry, who is just along for the ride, hangs from the side of the truck and pulls the lever whenever Simon tells him to.

> HENRY
>
> So I was a janitor! So what?

> SIMON
>
> But Angus James said he didn't even know you!

Henry shrugs and qualifies . . .

> HENRY
>
> Well, I mean, we weren't like bosom buddies or anything. But we used to talk sometimes. In the elevator. In the morning. He said he liked my ideas. Being a janitor's a good job if you're a writer. Especially the night shift; all that time to think and develop my ideas.

> SIMON
>
> Do it.

Henry pulls the lever and the garbage gets crushed.

Anyway, he hated my poem.

HENRY
Well, what the hell does he know? He wouldn't know a vital piece of literary art if it came up and bit him in the leg. To hell with him! He's not the only publisher in the world!

SIMON
But nobody likes it.

HENRY
(*smokes*)
It's true. A prophet is seldom heeded in his own land. Remember that.

SIMON
Do it.

Henry is about to pull the lever again, but sees something in amongst the garbage . . .

HENRY
Hey, look, treasure!

Henry steps down and leans over into the garbage. Simon joins him as he lifts something that is either a ring or a stray piece of machinery.

What is this?

SIMON
Brass maybe. Some kinda copper.

HENRY
It's a ring. Jewelry.

SIMON
I think it's a gasket. A fitting from off of that old refrigerator over there.

Henry puts it in his pocket, satisfied and Simon jumps on the back of the truck as it turns the corner and rolls away. Henry starts to walk off in the opposite direction, but stops when he sees Pearl age seven.

EXT. VICKY'S HOUSE – DAY

Henry comes up the street with Pearl age seven on his back. He walks into Vicky's yard and finds Warren lifting weights in the garage.

> HENRY
>
> Hey, Warren, I found Pearl wandering around by the garbage dump.

> WARREN
>
> He lost.

> HENRY
>
> Who lost?

Warren rests. He sits up on the bench and takes a toke off the joint he has waiting.

> WARREN
>
> Congressman Feer.

> HENRY
> (*realizing*)
>
> Oh. Well, you know. Somebody's gotta lose.

> WARREN
>
> What's the fucking use. You make sacrifices. You try to be a decent human being. Try to contribute something meaningful to society. And what happens? They lose to a bunch of cultural elite liberal fuck-ups. I don't give a shit anymore. People deserve what they get.

Henry pauses, then leads Pearl age seven towards the house. Warren lies back down and continues his lifting.

INT. VICKY'S HOUSE – DAY

Moments later.

Henry knocks on the door as he enters . . .

> HENRY
>
> Vicky?

No answer. He comes in and finds her sitting on the couch with a drink. She's got a black eye.

What happened to you?

VICKY
He's a good man, Henry. Nobody's perfect.

HENRY
I guess not.

VICKY
He's terribly disappointed.

HENRY
I found Pearl wandering around with no shoes on her feet.

Pearl comes over and stands beside her mother.

VICKY
Thanks. She gets scared.

HENRY
And you don't?

Vicky caresses Pearl's hair, then drinks and looks over at Henry.

VICKY
I love him.

INT. WORLD OF DONUTS – DAY

Moments later.

Buñuel is waiting when Henry walks in and steps up to the beer cooler.

HENRY
(*alarmed*)
Where's the beer?

MR DENG
No more beer. Coffee. Espresso! Cappuccino! Café au lait. Carrot juice. Herbal tea.

Henry looks at the man, disgusted, then falls in to a seat and motions to Gnoc, who is now the waitress.

HENRY

A double espresso and a jelly donut, Gnoc.
                    (*to Buñuel*)
You mind paying? My credit's no good here anymore,
apparently.

BUÑUEL

(*nods amiably*)
Did you go to the employment agency today, Henry?

HENRY

No, but it's OK. Simon's gunna try to get me a job on the
garbage truck.

BUÑUEL

Listen, I'm a little concerned about your friend.

HENRY

Simon?

BUÑUEL

Seems he gave an obscene note to a girl in the library.

HENRY

Get outta here! When?

BUÑUEL

I'm not sure.

HENRY

It couldn't have been Simon.

BUÑUEL

It almost certainly is. He mentions you. Look . . .

*He unfolds a print-out of the letter. Henry reads and Buñuel leans over,
pointing out . . .*

HENRY

'Her figure makes me violent. I want to somehow break her.
But tenderly. How is this possible? Ask Henry.'

*Henry thinks this over, gulps back some espresso and nods his approval.
Then . . .*

Buñuel, this is obviously a love letter.

                    BUÑUEL
                 (*taking it back*)
We've had complaints.

                    HENRY
Where did you get it?

                    BUÑUEL
She posted it on the Internet.

                    HENRY
Oh, the slut!

                    BUÑUEL
She was trying to warn other girls about a potential rapist.

                    HENRY
                  (*smokes*)
Is all this true about the Internet? About how you can get
pornography on it?

                    BUÑUEL
Well, yeah, sure. It's a big problem. You can send dirty
pictures and everything.

                    HENRY
On the Internet?

                    BUÑUEL
Yeah.

Henry is impressed.

                    HENRY
No kiddin'?

Buñuel gets up to go.

                    BUÑUEL
See you on Thursday, Henry.

                    HENRY
                  (*thinking*)
Sure. See you.

(*calls the waitress*)
Gnoc, gimme one of these double espressos to go, will ya?

He is having ideas.

INT. THE GRIM HOUSE KITCHEN – DAY

Moments later.

Fay, still dressed in black, is tapping away on the keys to the computer, surfing the Internet, as Henry appears at the kitchen door, gripping his tall double espresso.

> HENRY

Hello, Fay.

> FAY

Go away.

> HENRY

You gotta get outta the house, Fay. You can't blame yourself for not being here. You did all you could for her.

She turns and glares at him.

> FAY

Is there something you want?

Henry stops, pauses, looks away. Then . . .

> HENRY

You got the Internet on that contraption?

> FAY
> (*resumes typing*)

Yeah. So what?

He changes the subject again, preoccupied and continues tenderly . . .

> HENRY

Look Fay, about, you know, between us – what happened . . .

> FAY

I don't wanna talk about it, Henry!

He sighs and drinks his coffee, then looks back at her.

                    HENRY
Type a part of Simon's poem onto the Internet.

                    FAY
                  (*stops*)
What?

                    HENRY
Go ahead.

                    FAY
No.

                    HENRY
Why not?

                    FAY
Because.

                    HENRY
Come on, Fay. It's a great idea.

                    FAY
I don't know if he would want us to do that.

                    HENRY
Sure he would. Just the first ten verses.

Fay is tempted.

                    FAY
I don't know.

                    HENRY
He'll thank you for it later.

Frowning, she reconsiders. She gets up and takes the notebooks from the cabinet above the fridge. She flips through the pages but suddenly stops and turns to the door with a nicer attitude.

                    FAY
Henry . . .

But he's gone. It's as if he has vanished into thin air. She sighs, sits back down, and begins typing the poem onto the Internet.

INT. WORLD OF DONUTS – DAY

Moments later.

Henry comes back into the store, satisfied with himself. He finishes off his coffee, tosses away the cup and takes a pornographic magazine from the rack. He leans on the counter where Mr Deng is busy working and flips through the pages.

> HENRY
> Gimme another one of those tall double espressos, Mr Deng.

Mr Deng starts to make him one and sees him with the magazine.

> MR DENG
> You gunna buy that?

> HENRY
> I'm just looking.

> MR DENG
> Well then put it back.

> HENRY
> There's this fascinating story about a famous rock band and how they tied a friend of theirs to a bed in their hotel room and inserted a live fish into her vagina.

Mr Deng shakes his head and frowns.

> (*explains*)
> They say she had numerous orgasms.

> MR DENG
> Henry, you need to do something with your life. Get a job, or something.

> HENRY
> I mean, it wasn't the entire fish, it was just, you know, the nose. The nose of the fish.

Mr Deng brings over the coffee. Henry is surprised to notice he is not riveted.

> You don't find that interesting?

MR DENG

No.

Henry closes the magazine and puts it back. Leaning on the counter, he sips his coffee and ponders.

HENRY

You ever wonder what it would be like to have sex with an animal, Mr Deng?

MR DENG

That coffee is free. Just take it and get out of here.

HENRY

I mean, some dogs are almost as big as people and often more attractive.

Mr Deng just goes back to work, leaving Henry there at the counter thinking big thoughts.

EXT. THE GRIM HOUSE – EVENING

Simon hangs from the garbage truck as it comes up the street and pauses in front of his house. He jumps down and the truck barrels away.

INT. FAY'S ROOM – EVENING

Simon taps at the door. She looks over at him and he sees she's been crying. He comes into the room and she sits up on the edge of the bed.

SIMON

Did you see him?

FAY

He came by this afternoon.

SIMON

Did you talk?

FAY

No.

He comes over and sits beside her. He thinks a moment, then . . .

SIMON

You've got to tell him, Fay.

FAY

He thinks I'm a slut.

And she starts crying again. Simon awkwardly touches her shoulder, then moves his hand away. Fay pulls herself together, sniffles and goes into the bathroom.

INT. THE GRIM HOUSE, AT THE PIANO

Moments later.

Simon comes downstairs and finds Henry at the piano. He looks ill and is clutching a nearly empty container of espresso. He is staring sickly at 'the ring'.

SIMON

Henry?

HENRY

Simon, I don't feel so good.

SIMON

What's wrong?

HENRY

I feel all kinda clammy. And damp.

Simon lifts the coffee container and smells it.

SIMON

How many of these did you have?

Henry tries to remember. He squints.

HENRY

Seven.

Simon puts the container down and sits at the table.

SIMON

Henry, we have to talk.

HENRY

Can I use your toilet?

SIMON

Fay's taking a shower.

Henry grabs his stomach. He presses his hand against his chest, holds his head, then stares at the ring.

HENRY

How much you think I can get for this?

He looks at Simon.

SIMON
(pauses)

Henry, Fay's pregnant.

Henry looks at him.

Fay's pregnant with your child.

Henry lets this sink in. He stands and the room tilts. White with fear, he clutches at his rumbling gut.

INT. THE GRIM HOUSE BATHROOM

Moments later.

Fay is in the shower as . . .

Henry bursts into the bathroom, tearing at his belt and trousers. She starts screaming and wraps herself in the shower curtain. He drops his pants and throws himself on the toilet just in time to begin shitting his brains out. Fay crouches, terrified and disgusted, in the shower.

FAY

Jesus, Henry!

Henry sweats and moans as he empties his bowels in a violent and messy blast of noise and foul air.

Fay covers her face and whimpers sickly.

Finally, he's done. He hangs with his face out over his knees, sick, exhausted and in shock. Fay wraps herself in a towel and steps out of

107

the shower. She creeps carefully around him and flushes the toilet, growing increasingly concerned.

Hey, Henry. You OK?

He is destroyed, staring down at . . .

The 'ring' he still holds in his hand.

Fay sees this, looks at Henry, then kneels and takes it from him. He doesn't resist. She lifts it up and breathlessly admires it. Totally misunderstanding, moved beyond words . . .

Oh. Oh, Henry.

And she throws her arms around him as he sits there, sweating and spent, on the toilet.

INT. CHURCH – DAY

A month later.

Mr Deng and Buñuel drag Henry, kicking and screaming, into the church foyer. Once inside, he shakes them off and they stand back. He huffs and puffs and tosses the hair back out of his eyes. He paces back and forth like a caged animal, then stops, sees . . .

Fay, at the altar, waiting with Simon. She is beautiful.

Henry calms down, deeply affected.

Fay smiles down the aisle at him.

Henry throws back his shoulders, straightens his tie and strides up the aisle.

Also present at the ceremony are Vicky and Warren. Gnoc is maid of honor.

INT. CHURCH – DAY

Later.

Henry holds Fay's hand and repeats after Father Hawkes.

FATHER HAWKES

I, Henry, take you, Fay to be my wife.

HENRY

I, Henry, take you, Fay to be my wife.

FATHER HAWKES

And do promise before God and these witnesses . . .

HENRY

And do promise before God and these witnesses . . .

FATHER HAWKES

To be your loving and faithful husband.

HENRY

To be your loving and faithful husband.

FATHER HAWKES

In plenty and in want.

HENRY

In plenty and in want.

FATHER HAWKES

In joy and in sorrow.

HENRY

In joy and in sorrow.

FATHER HAWKES

In sickness and in health.

HENRY

In sickness and in health.

FATHER HAWKES

For as long as we both shall live.

HENRY

For as long as we both shall live.

The gasket everyone is now mistaking for a ring is lifted high before the altar.

Bless, O Lord, this ring, that he who gives it and she who wears it may abide in your peace and continue in your favor until their life's end.

The gasket is placed on Fay's finger.

Whom God has joined, let no man separate.

The doors of the church swing open with a tremendous creak and everyone turns from the altar to see . . .

Amy enter. She steps in and stands there, alarmed, clutching a long scroll of fax paper.

HENRY

Oh, shit.

FAY

Simon, do something.

Simon walks down the aisle to see to Amy.

The guests watch and wait.

As Simon reaches her, Amy looks away from the altar and shows him the fax scroll.

AMY

Look.

He studies the fax and recognizes his poem. He grows concerned.

SIMON

Where did you get this?

AMY

It's all over the Internet.

Simon looks up the aisle at . . .

Fay and Henry. They look away, caught.

They're even talking about it on the TV news.

Confused, Simon starts for the door, shoving the fax in his pocket. Fay steps down from the altar . . .

Simon?

Amy hurries along beside him.

There's a guy from the radio station over at World of Donuts and a story in the newspaper about some kids burning down a school near Boston!

INT. THE GRIM HOUSE – NIGHT

Later that evening.

The whole neighborhood is celebrating Fay's wedding. The music is loud. The people are drunk. The place is a shambles. A big dance number is playing. Amidst all the festivities, though, Simon and Buñuel have the small TV propped up on top of the fridge, following the evening news . . .

REPORTER
(*on TV*)

It all started right here in Queens, Jim, at World of Donuts about one year ago today, when local garbage man, Simon Grim, put pencil to paper and began to compose what many have come to regard as viscious, antisocial and pornographic poetry – 112 lines of unrhymed free meter verse which would one day serve to spark the flames of controversy across the nation and – indeed – the world.

Fay leads the neighbors in the dance . . .

OWEN FEER
(*on TV*)

This is outrageous! Measures must be taken. Have we debased our culture to such an extent that a garbage man with a head full of sick ideas is legitimately referred to as a poet, and where the filth he spews can be accessed by any child old enough to turn on a computer? Is this what we have come to? Not the transmission of our highest ideals, but a cynical, atheistic delirium!

Henry and Fay dance, surrounded by the dancing neighbors . . .

POET LAUREATE
(*on TV*)
Poetry of this kind, and this poem in particular, is, I think, a
worthy form of desperation; a digression on the extremes of
human experience; of solitude, of community. It is perhaps
alarming, even upsetting to some – myself included – but it
must be allowed to exist.

*Henry throws an arm around Warren, who stands looking dejected in
the doorway, and raises his glass to the happiness in the room.*

ANCHORMAN
(*on TV*)
Meanwhile, in Rome today, the Pope issued a message of
hope for believers in their fight against what he termed the
godless and lost. He did not mention Simon Grim by name,
but offered a prayer for the young whom he described as sadly
in need of faith and not the illusion of conviction offered by
rock music, drugs and contemporary poetry.

*The TV is switched off. It's later now. People are passed out on the
kitchen floor and various neighbors are sitting around the table. Fay
steps back from the TV, drains a glass of beer and wipes her mouth on
the sleeve of her wedding gown. She hugs Simon, who is deeply unsettled
by the news of his growing infamy.*

FAY
God, Simon, I mean, like, you're a total fucking rock star.

INT. WORLD OF DONUTS – DAY

*A huge crowd of kids are pressed up against the doors, trying to get a
peek at their hero, Simon Grim.*

*Angus comes away from the window. He stands and regards Simon,
who is sitting at a table tearing a napkin to shreds.*

ANGUS
I'm willing to negotiate, Simon.

SIMON
I know, it's just . . .

113

                    ANGUS
You've had other offers.

                    SIMON
Well, yes. But.

                    ANGUS
What?

                    SIMON
Why have you reconsidered?

                    ANGUS
Because I think your writing will be tremendously successful.

                    SIMON
But you don't like it?

                    ANGUS
It's growing on me.

                    SIMON
What made you change your mind?

He points to the fans outside.

                    ANGUS
Other people's responses. I don't live in a vacuum, you know.
Two months ago I didn't have the proof of your poem's
appeal. Now I do.

*Simon thinks this over, but says nothing. Angus comes over and lays his
hand on his shoulder.*

Consider my offer carefully. Get some professional advice. I'll
call you tomorrow.

Simon nods.

EXT. WORLD OF DONUTS – DAY

Moments later.

*Angus emerges and has to fight his way through the throng of excited
adolescents. He reaches his limo and gets in. But he pauses before closing
the door and considers the crowd.*

Simon emerges from the store and kids begin screaming and shouting for autographs. Angus shakes his head, impressed.

INT. CHURCH – DAY

Simon consults Father Hawkes.

> FATHER HAWKES
> What were the terms?

> SIMON
> A hundred thousand in cash up front.

> FATHER HAWKES
> Royalties?

> SIMON
> A seventy/thirty split.

> FATHER HAWKES
> Well, that could be better. But it is a hundred thousand dollars up front. Guaranteed money. You could use that.

> SIMON
> So it's a good deal?

> FATHER HAWKES
> Of course it's good.

> SIMON
> So I should take it?

> FATHER HAWKES
> No. Try to get him up to a hundred and fifty thousand.

EXT. JUNKYARD – DAY

Evening.

Henry stalks along, all fired up. Simon tries his best to keep up with him.

> HENRY
> I've let myself down, Simon! I've let myself be caught in the bloody maw of banal necessity! How did I get here? How did

this happen to me? I'm going to be somebody's father! I need time to think. To write. Time to finish my 'Confession'! I can't work for a living! It's impossible! I tried once. My genius will be wasted trying to make ends meet!

He collapses extravagantly.

This is how great men topple, Simon. Their hearts are in the right place too much of the time! They get sidetracked! Distracted. Oh! How could I have been so careless!

SIMON
Henry, please, let me read the 'Confession'.

HENRY
No. Not now. It's not done. I'm all washed up. I'm finished!

SIMON
Angus James is convinced my poem is going to make him incredibly wealthy. He'll read your book and seriously consider publishing it. If I ask him to. I'm certain.

Henry glances back at his friend, digesting this. He thinks it over, then . . .

HENRY
Really? You really think so?

Having finally got through to him, Simon comes forward, anxious to help Henry.

SIMON
I'll insist he publish the 'Confession'.

He paces back and forth, thrusting out his chest, for the first time in his life displaying something like pride or arrogance.

(*adds*)

Or I won't let him publish my poem.

Henry sits there watching Simon, impressed with this evidence of increased self-esteem. He realizes the profundity of the gesture.

HENRY
You'd do that? You'd do that for me?

116

Simon stares off into the distance.

> SIMON

You saved my life.

Henry is moved. He stands and comes forward. He grabs his friend by the shoulders and turns him around.

> HENRY

Do you realize what you're saying?

> SIMON
> (*pausing*)

I owe you everything.

Henry steps away, considering, then looks back at Simon and extends his hand.

> HENRY

OK.

Simon smiles. Henry smiles. They shake hands.

INT. HENRY'S APARTMENT – DAY

Simon enters, comes forward into the room and pauses, looking off at . . .

The stack of twelve books that comprise the 'Confession'.

EXT. HOUSE/BACKYARD – DAY

Henry stands outside, watching his door.

INT. HENRY'S APARTMENT – DAY

Simon lifts the first volume, opens it and begins reading. He sits.

EXT. BACKYARD – DAY

Henry paces, drinking and smoking nervously.

INT. HENRY'S APARTMENT – NIGHT

Simon strides the length of the living room, reading. He stops, frowns, then laughs. But his laughter dissolves into a look of confusion and he sits on the floor beside the fire.

EXT. BACKYARD – NIGHT

Henry crouches down and peeks in through the basement window, spying on Simon. Mr Deng arrives with more beer and joins the vigil.

INT. HENRY'S APARTMENT – NIGHT

Simon reads in front of the fire.

EXT. BACKYARD/GARAGE – NIGHT

Buñuel, Hawkes and Mr Deng sleep sitting up as Henry talks to himself. Fay leans out the back door and interrupts him. He looks at her, but says nothing. She sighs and goes back inside: turning off the lights.

INT. HENRY'S APARTMENT – DAY

The next morning.

Simon sits wearily reading the final page of volume twelve as the morning sun streaks into the room. Finally, he finishes and slowly closes the book. He stands and crosses the room. Leaning against the wall, he removes his glasses and rubs his aching eyes.

EXT. BACKYARD – DAY

Simon steps out of Henry's apartment and sees Henry asleep on the back stoop.

EXT. WORLD OF DONUTS – DAY

Simon stares into a glass of water. Fay sits ten feet away, waiting. Finally . . .

> FAY
>
> It's really that bad?

> SIMON
>
> It's terrible.

FAY

Maybe your expectations were too high. Are you sure you've
been objective?

*He just lifts his head and looks at her. This shuts her up. He drops his
head back down and sighs.*

INT. ANGUS JAMES' OFFICE – DAY

The 'Confession' lies on the big desk. Angus' hand comes down upon it.

ANGUS

You've read this?

SIMON

Yes.

ANGUS

And you want me to consider publishing it?

SIMON

Yes.

ANGUS

As part of our deal?

Yes.

ANGUS

Simon, this book, it's . . . It's really quite bad.

SIMON

That's what you said about my poem.

Angus pauses and figures. He changes the subject.

ANGUS

I'm offering you a very real expression of my faith in your
writing. Two hundred thousand dollars and a sixty/forty split.

SIMON

But just exactly what is the nature of your faith in my writing?

ANGUS

Look, Simon, you don't require my admiration. You require
my experience as a publisher. And that experience leads me
to believe your poem will make more money than any book of
poetry ever published. In history. Virtually make you a
household name within two years. You'll never have to work
on a garbage truck again, I assure you. Or do anything else for
that matter. Whereas this 'Confession' by Henry Fool . . .

He is at a loss for words.

The most I can say for this is . . . The man is a scoundrel.

SIMON

He taught me everything I know.

ANGUS

No! He encouraged all that was expressive in you to become
manifest. He inspired you to act. He influenced your
perception.

Simon waits a while, staring at his shoes.

SIMON

How about if my advance is only a hundred thousand?

ANGUS

It's not about money, Simon.

SIMON

We could split the royalties seventy/thirty.

ANGUS

I will not publish Henry Fool's 'Confession'.

Simon sits and lets this sink in. Angus waits, then . . .

Will you sign the contract?

Simon continues looking out at the city. Angus waits, but there is no response. Finally, Simon turns, pauses and slowly crosses the room.

He sits at the table and looks down at the contract.

He signs.

INT. THE GRIM HOUSE KITCHEN – DAY

Fay is in labor. Henry helps her into her coat as they rush for the door.

INT. WORLD OF DONUTS – DAY

Moments later.

Henry runs into the store and stands there, panicked, looking at Hawkes, Buñuel and Mr Deng. Gnoc runs out to get Fay.

EXT. WORLD OF DONUTS – DAY

Henry and Gnoc load Fay into the van. The van pulls out.

INT. VAN – DAY

Henry drives recklessly. Fay rolls around in the back.

INT. HOSPITAL CORRIDOR – DAY

Fay is in a wheelchair being rushed down the hall. She is gripping Henry's hand as he runs along beside her.

INT. HOSPITAL DELIVERY ROOM – DAY

Fay gasps and sweats as the Doctor and Nurse prepare her. She is scared. She looks over at . . .

Henry, looking in through the window. He looks scared too.

Fay is sedated by gas.

Henry is taken away by the Nurse.

Fay stares up at the ceiling.

INT. HOSPITAL WAITING ROOM – NIGHT

Henry is asleep on a row of waiting-room chairs, exhausted.

Simon comes running up the hall and finds him. It's late and no one is around. He sits down beside Henry and shakes him.

Henry wakes.

HENRY
Simon? You're here.

He sits up and Simon sits beside him.

SIMON
What happened?

HENRY
(*coughs*)

It's a boy.

SIMON

And Fay?

HENRY

She's alright.

Simon sits back, relieved. Then he remembers the rain-soaked shopping bag he has with him. He pulls out a couple of cans of beer and hands one to Henry.

Thanks.

They look around, seasoned conspirators and make sure the coast is clear. Then they pop open the beers and toast.

They drink. Then . . .

How did it go?

Simon pauses, scared, then gets up and crosses the room. He looks out of the window and gathers his strength.

SIMON
Listen, Henry, Angus James didn't like your 'Confession'.

Henry looks at Simon blankly, then blinks and looks away.

HENRY
Ah. I see. Well, what now?

SIMON
What do you mean?

HENRY
Did he suggest changes?

Silence. Simon comes back and sits again.

SIMON
No. He didn't.

HENRY

I mean, after all, there are things I can do to make it more
accessible.

SIMON

Accessible?

HENRY

I can soften up some of the language and make it read easier.
Take out some of the more intratextual references and
popularize the underlying *Sturm und Drang*, so to speak. I can
change its mode. Make it more of a conventional novel
instead.

Simon just stares at him blankly, then sighs and shakes his head.

SIMON

No. Don't.

HENRY
(*laughing*)
Oh, Simon, don't be such a purist! I appreciate your
protectiveness, but the integrity of the work gives it a
durability that can sustain such things.

Simon comes over and lays his hand on Henry's shoulder.

SIMON

No. Really, Henry. Don't.

HENRY

What are you saying; that it doesn't merit revision?

SIMON

I'm saying . . . Angus James didn't like it.

*He steps away and sits. Henry pauses, then approaches and leans down
over him.*

HENRY

Well, did you tell him what you think?

SIMON

What I think doesn't matter.

HENRY

Yes, it does. You've got to use your influence with him.

SIMON

I gave it to him to read and he hated it. What more can I do?

HENRY

You can refuse to let him publish your poem.

SIMON

I can't do that.

HENRY

You said you would.

SIMON

That was before I read your book.

HENRY
(*hit hard*)

Oh.

SIMON
(*looking up at him*)

I signed the contract, Henry.

Henry stands there a moment longer, then lowers himself into the nearest seat, weakened.

Look, Henry, what did you expect?

HENRY

I . . . I don't know. Honesty, perhaps.

SIMON
(*indignantly*)

Look, if I had told you, when at first I read it, that I thought it was no good, what would you have done?

HENRY

I would have respected your opinion.

SIMON

And insisted that there's no accounting for taste.

HENRY

Well, is there?

Simon's words catch in his throat. He turns away, frustrated.

SIMON

I don't know. I didn't bring it to Angus because I thought it was good. I brought it to Angus because you're my friend.

HENRY
(*staggered*)

Oh how perfectly enormous of you, Simon.

SIMON
(*explodes*)

Look, Henry, I did it! I wrote. I wrote poetry because you told me to! I worked! I worked while you sat back and comfortably dismissed the outside world as too shallow, stupid and mean to appreciate your ideas.

HENRY

Is that such a priority? Is that some sort of measure of a man's worth? To drag what's best in him out into the street so every average slob with some pretense to taste can poke it with a stick?

SIMON
(*sits, tired*)

Maybe. Maybe it is.

Henry just stares at him, stands, then turns on his heel and waves him off.

HENRY

You must be pretty impressed with yourself, huh? The all too obviously talented new man, the important new voice, the early clue to a new direction, or whatever, etc., etc., etc! A popular new trend conveniently packaged for the distracted young herd! You want to be liked more than you know, Simon Grim! You'd be nowhere without me and you know it.

Simon hangs his head, destroyed.

I'm leaving.

Henry is scared all of a sudden. But he puts on a defiant exterior.

HENRY

Yes. It's time you left.

He stands, drinks and walks over to the window . . .

I saw you for what you were in the beginning, Simon. I hold no grudge and I'm certain you will, in time, leave some serious and small dent in this world.

SIMON
(*weakly*)

The world is full of shit.

Henry take advantage of Simon's disillusionment and puts on a big show of secure wisdom.

HENRY

The world is full of shit. It's true. And you have to walk through it. That's your part. I'm sorry. But you're no good at it. Perhaps I'm not. Perhaps I wasn't made to walk through shit. Go on now. Leave. Do what you're good at. Go.

Simon sits there a moment, numb with grief. Henry, red in the face, stares at the floor. Suddenly, Simon stands and walks out. Henry looks up and watches him go. He can hardly believe it. He almost raises his voice and apologizes, but can't. He lowers his head again and covers his face with his hands, listening to Simon's footsteps receding through the halls.

Simon walks on, away from us, down the hospital corridor.

FADE TO BLACK

EXT. STREET – DAY

Seven years later.

Fay bangs out of the kitchen door with her seven-year-old son Ned. Frazzled and overworked, she grips a loaded laundry basket to her side as she sits Ned down on the curb and points at him.

FAY

Play!

The kid sits still, obviously guilty of some unspeakable mischief, as Fay storms back into the house. He looks around, bored, then brightens up when he sees . . .

Henry, coming up the street, hanging from the back of a garbage truck.

INT. THE INFERNO – DAY

Moments later.

Henry enters with Ned on his back and the bartender, Patty, goes ballistic.

PATTY

Henry, what did I tell you about bringing the kid in here!

HENRY

Say hello to Patty, Ned.

NED

Hi.

She suddenly becomes all soft and cuddly.

PATTY

How you doin', sweetie? You wanna Coke?

He nods and Henry stands him on a stool at the bar.

HENRY

So what did you learn at school today, Ned? Anything?

He shakes his head.

Here, I'll teach you something.

He hands Ned a cigarette and lights it for him. Ned takes a drag and coughs.

Horrible, isn't it?

Ned nods in agreement.

NED

It burns.

HENRY

See. That'll teach ya. Here, sip this.

And he offers the kid his whiskey.

EXT. THE GRIM HOUSE – DAY

Same time.

Fay comes out of the house and looks for her son.

FAY

Ned!

She comes out to the street and looks around.

Ned!

EXT. VICKY'S HOUSE – DAY

Fay comes up looking for Ned and sees . . .

Pearl, age fourteen, come out of Vicky's House. She is fourteen years old now. Warren steps out the door and grabs her by the arm. She shakes him off. He slaps her.

She runs down the steps and glares back at him.

WARREN

(*pointing at her*)

I'm warning you, Pearl!

Pearl turns defiantly away and walks into the street.

INT. THE INFERNO – DAY

Same time.

Henry is teaching Ned how to tip a topless dancer. A dancer stands on the bar and stretches her garter as Ned slips a dollar bill in beneath it.

HENRY

That's it. That's it. Perfect!

Some other guy down the bar is reading a newspaper . . .

BILL

Hey, Fool, it's about your friend – what's his name. Your brother-in-law.

Henry looks over. The guy, Bill, shows him the article.

HENRY

What about him?

BILL
(*reading*)

The controversial and reclusive American poet Simon Grim has been awarded the Nobel Prize in Literature. The Swedish Academy, who will confer the award late next week, praised Mr Grim for works of great and difficult striving, for the rendering of the desperate, the ugly and the mundane in a language packed with our shared human frailties . . .

HENRY

God, they must be hard up for geniuses to pin medals on because, listen, I gotta tell you, when I first met this guy he didn't even know what an iambic pentameter was.

BILL

He's a fraud.

HENRY

Keep a lid on it, Bill, you're outta your league.

BILL

Stir things up so as to stay in the newspapers. That's his racket.

HENRY

He's a great American poet, you dumb fuck!

BILL

Poet, my ass! I could puke all over a piece a loose leaf and be more profound than he is!

HENRY

Come over here and say that and I'll cripple ya in three

different ways, you boozed-up Philistine!

FAY

Henry!

Henry and Ned crouch and quiver – caught. Fay strides up to the bar and grabs the kid.

Listen, you degenerate, I've had about enough of this!
(*smells Ned's breath*)
Ned, have you been drinking?

The kid checks with Henry then looks back at Fay and nods. Fay looks at her husband, outraged.

HENRY
(*explains*)
His throat hurt from smoking.

Fay slaps him across the face – hard – and the place goes quiet. Henry shakes his head clear and she pokes him in the chest with her finger.

FAY
Henry, don't come home tonight! I'm warning you! Don't come home at all! Ever!

And she storms out with the kid. Henry snaps his jaw back into place, then looks at Patty and Bill and shrugs. He knocks back his drink and motions for another.

EXT. WORLD OF DONUTS – NIGHT

Later (evening).

Henry staggers out of the back door of the Inferno and comes across Mr Deng sitting against the wall of the store, watching the basketball game on a small TV. World of Donuts vibrates with loud music.

HENRY

Who's winning?

MR DENG

Nobody.

Henry gestures to World of Donuts . . .

131

HENRY

What's going on in there?

MR DENG

We gotta have rock 'n' roll shows these days, Henry. The poetry readings just don't pay the bills no more.

HENRY

What did I tell you! It was just a fad. I told you that! I told everyone!

MR DENG

Did you hear about Simon? It was on the news today.

HENRY

Yeah yeah yeah. So what? A Nobel Prize. Anybody can get one of them these days. That's the problem, with this world, Mr Deng . . . Nobody's got any standards anymore. You seen Fay?

MR DENG

You better sleep in my office tonight, Henry. She was very angry. You've gotta let her cool off.

HENRY

I can't sleep in there with that racket!

MR DENG

Suit yourself.

Henry considers his options, then . . .

INT. GARAGE – NIGHT

The place is abandoned.

Henry comes in and, just as he is laying down to go to sleep on an old couch, finds Pearl age fourteen.

She is hardened and disturbed, but frequently vulnerable and scared; a troubled kid.

HENRY

What are you doing here, Pearl?

PEARL

You want some?

HENRY
(*pauses*)

Some what?

Pearl comes towards him. He is kneeling with his face at her crotch level when she reaches him. She holds out a bottle of cheap rot-gut wine. Realizing, he takes it and drinks. He winces.

Shit!

Pearl laughs and falls back onto the couch, her sweater hanging off her shoulder and her skirt hiked up and displaying her underwear.

Henry stands and searches for something to sit on.

PEARL

Come sit here.

She pats the couch beside her.

He comes over, eyeing her carefully and sits. He hands back the bottle. She drinks, winces and sits staring at the flames.

That's what my dad always says.

HENRY

What?

PEARL
(*dead*)

'You want some?'

Henry looks away, uncomfortable. She slides her gaze over to him, their eyes meet, and she pins him to the spot.

People say you were once in jail for having sex with a girl my age.

HENRY

That was a long time ago.

He gets up and stands at the window. Pearl age fourteen watches him closely as she drinks, then . . .

133

PEARL

You want some?

He looks over at her and she slides her coat off her shoulder. Henry is sweating.

HENRY

You oughta get outta here, Pearl.

PEARL

I was here first.

HENRY

Go home.

PEARL

You go home.

HENRY

Fine.

And he starts to leave. But Pearl sits up . . .

PEARL
(scared)

Wait!

Henry stops and looks back at her.

(hanging her head)

I can't go home.

HENRY
(concerned)

Why not?

PEARL

He beat her up again.

Henry holds his head, tries to sober up. He looks around the room, then focuses on the girl.

HENRY

Warren beat up your mom?

Pearl stares at the floor. She glances over at him, then back down at the bottle gripped in her hands. She nods.

Henry pauses, then comes across the room, lowering himself tentatively to the couch.

Is she alright?

She says nothing for a moment, then . . .

> PEARL
> (*sadly*)

Do you think I'm pretty?

Henry lifts his hand and covers his face. He looks up at the ceiling and sighs. He returns to Pearl . . .

> HENRY

Does she need help?

Pearl reaches over and grabs his thigh. Looking up at him, with tears rolling down her face, she suggests . . .

> PEARL

I'll suck your cock if you kill him for me.

Henry jumps away from her and Pearl throws herself down on the couch, covering her face.

INT. VICKY'S HOUSE – NIGHT

Moments later.

Henry barges in and starts searching for . . .

> HENRY

Vicky! Vicky, it's Henry from across the street! Vicky!

He runs through the house, checking the rooms. He throws open the door to the bedroom and finds . . .

Vicky, sitting on the edge of the bed, smoking. She has a black eye and a swollen cheek.

> (*taken back*)

Vicky?

VICKY
(*standing*)
What do you think you're doing, you idiot!

WARREN
(*off*)
Hey!

Henry looks over and sees Warren stumble drunkenly out of the bathroom.

What are you doing in my house?

HENRY
(*to Vicky*)
It's about Pearl.

Vicky looks troubled. She sits back down with a sigh.

VICKY
Mind your own business, Henry.

WARREN
(*shoves him*)
Yeah, who the hell do you think you are, anyway?

Henry falls back and looks at Vicky. She looks away.

Henry looks at Warren, pauses, then gives him a sharp, hard shove.

Warren stands back against the wall, pauses, then erupts into visciousness.

He grabs Henry and throws him violently down the hall, where he hits the wall and collapses.

As Henry gets to his knees, Warren kicks him in the ribs. Henry curls up and rolls out on to the kitchen floor. Warren kicks him in the side of the head.

Vicky sits back down on the bed, covering her ears.

Warren beats the hell out of Henry, kicking him in the face and ribs whenever he manages to get up on his hands and knees. Henry crawls under the kitchen table for safety. Warren grabs his feet and drags him

136

out. As he is dragged across the floor, Henry finds a screwdriver and grabs it. He rolls over on his back as . . .

Warren lunges down at him again and . . .

WARREN
Ah.

Warren is stabbed in the heart.

Henry can't believe it.

Warren can't believe it. He stands there in the middle of the kitchen, amazed, with the screwdriver sticking out of his chest.

Henry, semi-conscious and severely beaten, falls against the back door and coughs up a few of his teeth. Vicky steps into the hall from her room and shudders.

Warren sits at the table, stunned. He looks from the screwdriver to Vicky, then . . .

Fuck.

He falls to the floor.

EXT. STREETS – NIGHT

Henry staggers away, limping. He comes to the intersection at the end of the block and doesn't know which way to run. Panicked, he looks round, holding his arm to his chest. He runs towards the highway.

INT. POLICE STATION – NIGHT

Later.

Fay is wired beyond belief. Trying to listen attentively, but still too overwhelmed to maintain her concentration.

LAWYER
(*off*)
It is true your husband served seven years in prison for statutory rape.

                            FAY
Yes. It is.

                          LAWYER
And when was that?

                            FAY
That was . . . I dunno. Fifteen . . . Sixteen years ago.

                          LAWYER
And when were you married?

                            FAY
We were married seven years ago.

                          LAWYER
Were you aware at all of the victim's relationship with his
daughter?

                            FAY
Pardon me?

                          LAWYER
The girl, the daughter, Pearl. She had been having sexual
relations with her father.

Fay is overwhelmed.

                            FAY
I didn't know that. No.

                          LAWYER
Pearl claims she offered your husband sexual favors if he
would kill her father.

*Fay just looks at him blankly, overwhelmed, confused. She starts to cry
quietly.*

I'm just repeating what she said, Mrs Fool. The victim's wife,
Vicky, claims your husband broke into the house and
forcefully entered her bedroom.

*Fay trembles and catches her breath trying to take this all in. A cop
hands her some tissues. She takes them and tries to concentrate on what
the lawyer says.*

                            138

Fay, I know this isn't easy. But we need your help here. The girl claims she asked your husband to kill her father in exchange for, well, I guess the promise of sexual relations with her.

INT. POLICE STATION CORRIDOR – NIGHT

Later.

Fay staggers out into the noisy corridor and rests against the wall. Looking down the hall she sees . . .

Pearl and Vicky, sitting in a blank, brightly lit room beyond a glass door.

Fay comes closer and looks in at them.

They don't see her. They stare at the floor before them, dazed and confused.

INT. THE GRIM HOUSE – DAY

Morning.

Fay is lying on her bed with her coat still on, trying to think. Ned stands by the side of the bed, watching her.

                                NED

Mom?

                                FAY

Yeah.

                                NED

Where's Dad?

                                FAY

I don't know, honey. Leave me alone a minute, I gotta think.

He picks at the bedspread and looks at the ceiling, then . . .

                                NED

Mom?

                                FAY

What!

NED

Is Dad in trouble?

FAY

Yes, Ned, he is. He's in big trouble. Now just be quiet for
two minutes.

*He walks around to the other side of the bed and waits a moment
before . . .*

NED

Mom?

FAY

I'm warning you, Ned.

NED

Mom, can I be a mailman when I grow up?

Fay sits up, pauses and studies her son.

FAY

Sure you can, honey. You can be anything you want.

*Ned is happy to hear this. He shuffles out of the room and Fay falls
back on the bed.*

INT. THE GRIM HOUSE KITCHEN — DAY

Moments later.

Ned comes into the kitchen and digs through the drawers beneath the sink. He finds an envelope. He reads the return address: Chelsea Hotel, New York City.

EXT. SUBWAY — DAY

Ned approaches the subway station and climbs the stairs to the platform.

EXT. SUBWAY PLATFORM — DAY

Moments later.

Ned runs up the stairs to the elevated platform just as a train pulls into the station. He runs down a few cars and hops in as the doors slide open.

INT. TRAIN — DAY

Ned rides the train to New York City.

EXT. SUBWAY STOP — DAY

Twenty minutes later.

He comes up out of the subway on to the street, looks around.

INT. HOTEL LOBBY — DAY

He comes into the hotel and rings an annoying buzzer which brings out the concierge, who is in his little office, watching TV.

                         CONCIERGE
    Yeah, what do you want?

                              NED
    My uncle.

                         CONCIERGE
    What's his name?

                              NED
    Simon Grim.

The concierge looks through his book as Ned waits.

                          CONCIERGE
    There ain't no one here by that name.

*Ned pulls the envelope from his pocket, unfolds it and shows it to the
concierge.*

                              NED
    Room 423.

The concierge studies the envelope and hands it back.

                          CONCIERGE
    This is post marked five years ago.

*Disappointed, Ned takes back the envelope and stands looking at his
sneakers.*

    What does he look like?

                              NED
                          (*hopeless*)
    I don't know.

                          CONCIERGE
    Sorry, kid. Can't help ya.

*Ned steps away from the front desk and moves towards the door. But
then he stops and looks back at . . .*

*The concierge, sitting back in his office, returning his attention to the
TV set.*

The boy heads for the elevator.

The concierge looks up and sees him.

                          (*jumping up*)
    Hey!

Ned checks his step and runs for the service stairs.

The concierge goes after him.

INT. HOTEL STAIRCASE – DAY

Moments later.

Ned runs up the stairs, the concierge in pursuit.

INT. HOTEL CORRIDOR – DAY

Moments later.

Ned jumps out into the hall, narrowly escaping the clutches of the concierge, who falls to the floor.

Ned runs up the hall, checking the room numbers as the concierge gets to his feet. He finds . . .

Room 423.

He knocks.

The concierge strides up the hall towards him.

Ned knocks again.

The concierge bears down upon him.

He knocks again and . . .

The door opens a crack, held by its safety chain. A female figure in silhouette is at the narrow gap.

Ned looks from the door to the concierge approaching.

The concierge arrives and reaches out for him, but the door opens wide and Ned dives in.

INT. HOTEL ROOM 423 – DAY

Same time.

The concierge stands in the hallway. The door swings shut in his face.

Ned kneels on the floor of the hotel room, waiting to be smacked, or something.

But when nothing happens, he opens his eyes and looks back over his shoulder at . . .

Laura, the secretary from the publishing house. She is dressed for travel and has her coat hung over her arm, a suitcase in her hand. She smiles at him, then looks from the boy to someone across the room and . . .

Ned follows her gaze to find . . .

Simon, standing there before him, a suitcase in his hand as well. He looks down at Ned with a calm, intrigued expression.

The boy looks up at him in awe.

Simon steps forward, pauses, then . . .

SIMON

Get up off your knees.

He does.

EXT. WORLD OF DONUTS – DAY

A taxi pulls up. Simon and Ned climb out and Laura leans out of the window.

LAURA

Promise me you'll be on that plane at seven, Simon.

SIMON

I'll see you in Stockholm.

They kiss. The taxi pulls away. Simon comes down beside Ned, takes the boy by the shoulders and whispers in his ear.

The kid takes off.

Simon looks over at World of Donuts and sees Gnoc waiting there at the door.

EXT. BEHIND WORLD OF DONUTS – DAY

Gnoc leads Simon out through the kitchen. A band is seen doing a sound check, inside.

Buñuel and Hawkes are waiting there, looking concerned.

Simon gives Buñuel his passport.

Buñuel nods and leaves.

Hawkes and Gnoc open the cellar doors.

INT. WORLD OF DONUTS BASEMENT – DAY

Moments later.

Simon is lead down the stairs and stops. He looks on in horror at . . .

Henry, lying on a makeshift bed, badly beaten up and weak. Mr Deng is wrapping his chest in bandages.

Simon pauses, then comes closer. He reaches out and touches Henry's shoulder, standing there looking down at his friend. Henry looks up at him, pauses and then gestures vaguely with his hand.

> HENRY
> Look, Simon, the world's a scary place. I admit it. But it's not my fault. I swear!

Simon thinks about this and looks away.

> SIMON
> I'm sorry, Henry.

> HENRY
> Don't be. You had things to do.

> SIMON
> So did you.

Henry thinks about that, sighs and looks away.

INT. THE GRIM HOUSE – DAY

Fay packs up the many books of the 'Confession' into one of the old suitcases Henry first came to town with. She slams it shut.

EXT. THE GRIM HOUSE – DAY

Ned runs along the street and stops at the police car. He points down the street with great urgency. The cops jump in their cars and take off. He then looks over at . . .

Fay, leaving the house with Henry's suitcase.

EXT. WORLD OF DONUTS BACK ALLEY – DAY

Same time.

Buñuel backs his car into the alley behind World of Donuts. Stepping out of the car he hands Simon back the passport.

Simon checks it and then looks up to see . . .

Father Hawkes and Mr Deng helping Henry outside. Coming out into the daylight, he straightens up and manages to walk on his own. He motions Ned over and leans down to the kid with difficulty.

                                    HENRY
     Gotta light?

Ned does. He has his own Zippo lighter and he proudly lights his dad's cigarette.

Henry smokes, hugs Ned, then leans back and pauses. Finally . . .

     Take care of your mom and don't start trouble you can't
     finish.

Ned nods and Henry pats him on the shoulder. Then he stands before Fay and looks at his feet. With her arms folded across her chest and her hip cocked, she taps her foot impatiently and waits for his last line of crap.

     I love you, Fay.

                                    FAY
                              (*rolls her eyes*)
     Yeah, well, tough.

But then she looks at him and softens. He leans in and kisses her passionately on the mouth.

Moments later, they all help Henry into Buñuel's car and Simon gets in behind the wheel. The doors slam shut and Simon steers the car slowly up the alley. Henry gazes out at Fay running along beside the car with the rest of the neighborhood, some of them laughing, some of them crying . . .

EXT. AIRPORT TERMINAL – DAY

Simon pulls up at the curb and jumps out. He helps Henry climb out and together they enter the terminal.

INT. AIRLINE TICKET COUNTER – DAY

Moments later.

Henry steps up.

> AIRLINE TICKET CLERK
> Passport and ticket, please.

Henry hands them over. He glances back at . . .

Simon, waiting.

The clerk compares Henry to the picture in the passport, checks again, then . . .

> (*recognizes*)
> It's an honor to meet you, Mr Grim. Really. I mean, God. Congratulations on the Nobel Prize.

                              HENRY
Thanks.

                        AIRLINE TICKET CLERK
I know all your work by heart. It changed my life.

                              HENRY
Yeah, well. Look, thanks, but . . .

                        AIRLINE TICKET CLERK
Yes. Of course.

She types something more into the computer, then looks up urgently.

You'll have to hurry, sir. They're holding the plane for you on
the runway.

INT. AIRPORT GATE – DAY

Moments later.

*Airline representatives come rushing up with walkie-talkies to meet
Henry and Simon as they run through the terminal.*

                        AIRLINE REP #1
This way, please, this way! This way, Mr Grim! This way!
Excuse me!

*As they are ushered up towards the gate, Henry stops and looks off at
the security guards and ground crew waiting for him, certain they can
spot him as a wanted criminal.*

                              SIMON
                           (*shoves him*)
Go on.

*Henry is ushered through security. They take his ticket and check his
passport again. They take his suitcase and place it on the conveyor belt.
He passes through the metal detector. They pass the metal detector wand
over him and he stands there with his hands outstretched, as . . .*

Simon waits and watches.

*The suitcase rolls out from the x-ray machine and as Henry grabs it, he
stops and looks across the security checkpoint at . . .*

Simon, standing there. He steps forward anxiously.

Henry lingers, speechless, but the airline representatives are at his side . . .

> AIRLINE REP
> Mr Grim, please, the plane is waiting! We have to hurry!

They drag him away, but Henry looks back as . . .

Simon stops and watches.

EXT. AIRPORT RUNWAY – DAY

Moments later.

The plane is waiting out on the asphalt and the airline representative runs straight for it, calling back over her shoulder to Henry . . .

> AIRLINE REP
> This way, Mr Grim! This way!

Runway technicians rush to their positions, but Henry hangs back and struggles across the tarmac, looking back over his shoulder at . . .

Simon, behind the huge plate glass window of the terminal.

He stops and waits.

Simon raises his hand in farewell and . . .

Henry raises his in reply.

Then Simon, unheard behind the gigantic glass wall, silent amongst the roar of the runway, says . . .

> SIMON
> (*unheard*)

Run.

And Henry understands. He lowers his hand, waits just a moment, then turns and looks out at . . .

The airplane. The airline representative is shouting at him from the foot of the stairs and waving him on with her walkie-talkie.

He glances back once more at Simon. Then . . .

Henry is running, struggling towards us, forcing himself towards the plane, getting stronger and running faster with every step he takes.

CUT TO BLACK

CREDITS

CONCIERGE	Paul Greco
COP #1	Blake Willett
COP #2	Raymond Cassar
AIRLINE TICKET CLERK	Katreen Hardt
FLIGHT ATTENDANT LUCY	Rebecca Nelson
ANGRY CUSTOMER	Paul Albe
TEENAGERS AT WORLD OF DONUTS	Vivian Bang
	Brandon Boey
	Claire Ritchie
	Herbie Duarte
	Toy Connor

CREW

Written, Directed and Produced by	Hal Hartley
Cinematography	Mike Spiller
Production Design	Steve Rosenzweig
Editing	Steve Hamilton
Production Manager	Matthew Myers
Associate Producers	Jerome Brownstein
	Thierry Cagianut
Executive Producers	Larry Meitrich
	Daniel J. Victor
	Keth Abell
Gaffer	W. F. Stubblefield
Best Boy Electric	Pamela Weese
3rd Electric	Joseph Stubblefield
Additional Electric	Teresa Ballard
Electric Intern	Aninna Furrer
1st Assistant Director	Richard Greenberg
2nd Assistant Director	Dena Gittelman
2nd 2nd Assistant Director	Michael Lerman
Script Supervisor	Adrienne Tien
Casting Coordinator	Chelsea Fuhrer
1st Assistant Camera	Storn (Norp) Peterson
2nd Assistant Camera	Bart Blaise
Camera Loader	Kim Alepin
Stills Photographer	Richard Sylvarnes
Camera Interns	Shelley Herbert
	Laura Hudock
Key Grip	Tim Kelly
Best Boy Grip	Terrence C. Burke

3rd Grip	Casey Campbell
Additional Grip	Rosie Vanek
Grip Production Assistant	John McNulty
Grip Intern	Nicholas Phillips
Grip Dog	Edie
Sound Mixer	Daniel McIntosh
Boom Operator	Karl Wasserman
Cable Person	Dave Raphael
Costume Designer	Jocelyn Joson
Costume Coordinator	Jacqueline Atkins
Wardrobe Intern	Rena (Michelle) Gleghorn
Key Make-Up & Hair	Claus Lulla
Assistant Make-Up & Hair	Sophia Jackson
Additional Make-Up & Hair	Hildie Ginsberg
Set Decorator	Melissa P. Lohman
Prop Master	Michael Zadrosny
Additional Props	Connie Van Flandern
Prop Production Assistant	Andrew Biscontini
Assistant to the Designer	Dania Saragovia
Art Production Assistants	Gerrit Gillis
	Jeremy Yoder
Art Interns	Jeffrey Cobb
	Theresa Dillon
	Bettina Oberli
	Ben Telford
Carpenters	Chris Sbrollini
	Mark Bailey
Location Manager	Andy Clark
Assistant Location Manager	Christine Welker
Location Assistant	Clara Bijl
Location Scout	Christie Mullen
Original Music Composed by	Hal Hartley
Arranged and Performed by	Hal Hartley & Jim Coleman
Additional Songs by	

RYFUL

Jim Coleman, Bill Dobrow
Hal Hartley, Lydia Kavanagh
Hub Moore

Production Office Coordinator	Elizabeth Ann Chae
Asst. Prod. Office Coordinators	Greer A. Burkholder
	Moon Cho
Production Accountant	Joyce Hsieh

Accounting Assistant	Michael Meere
Key Office Production Assistant	Susan Leber
Office Production Assistants	Ilona Cheshire
	Sara Rice
Production Office Interns	Laetita Saarbach
	Curtis Tsui
	Deirdre Waldron
	Josh Wick
Key Set Production Assistant	Zachary Jasie
Set Production Assistants	Jennie Dorosh
	Paul Echeverria Jones
	Blaire Lennane
	Paul McGuckin
	Dane Young
Additional Set Production Assistant	Ilona Cheshire
Additional Production Assistants	Sean Casey
	Leane Clifton
	Daniel Huber
	Brian Murphy
	Tim O'Connell
	Kent Zuber
Set Intern	Keith Hedlund
Production Interns	Josh Horowitz
	Pamela Watson
Caterer	Fresh Dish
	Stacey Goldstein
Craft Services	Charles Moss
Additional Craft Services	Elizabeth Klenk
Transportation Captain	Jim Buckman
Transportation Coordinator	Tom Weisler
Parking Coordinator	Jose Tesada
Parking Production Assistants	Sergio Arroyo
	Jose Candelario
	Sergio Cortina
	Lance McKinney
	Noel Rivera
Security Coordinator	Wayne Petrocelli
Security Guards	Bob Dibiase
	Christian Hackmack
	Thomas Hawk

True Fiction Pictures

Production Office Liaison	Kendall McCarthy
Comptroller	Ann Kulberg
Post-Production Interns	Jean Stehle
	Matteo A. Masiello
	Gautama Kavuri

The Shooting Gallery

Production Executives	Nancy Kriegel
	Brandon Rosser
Product Placement, Clearance &	
Promotions	Leonard John Bruno
	Leslie Lambert

Screenplay developed in association with Zenith Productions
Ltd., London
Thanks to
Scott Meek
Post-Production Services Provided by
Spin Cycle Post
New York City

Operations Manager	Jeanette King-Segnini
Assistant Editor	Seth E. Anderson
2nd Assistant Editor	Justine Halliday
Apprentice Editor	Rachel Chancey
Post-Production Supervisor	Matthew Myers
Re-Recording Engineer	Reilly Steele
Re-Recording Facilities	Sound One Corp.
Negative Matching	Nöelle Penraat
Color by	Du Art Film Laboratories
Color Timer	David Pultz
Dolby Sound Consultant	Tony V. Stevens

Titles Designed & Produced by
Rei Media Group
New York City

Legal Counsel	Rudolph & Beer, LLP
Payroll	Axium Payroll Services
Insurance	DISC Insurance
	North American Specialty Co.
Panaflex Cameras & Chapman	
Dolly Equipment	Panavision New York

Grip and Lighting Equipment	Lights in the Park, Inc.
	Xeno Lights, Inc.
	Broadway Studios
Production Vehicles	Budget Car & Truck Rental
	Looking Glass Associates, LP
Tutoring Service	On Location Education
Tutoring Coordinator	Alan Simon
Tutors	Amy Alson
	Gillian Kane
	Muriel Kester

Special thanks to

Gary Adriance, John Alex, Allied Insurance, Bangash Family, Glen
Basner, Christ Bieler, Steve Blakely, Lou Bonjovanni, Anthony Bregman,
Lisa Bruce, Kathy Carlis, Chase Manhattan, Circe's, Susan Clark, Eddy
Collyns, Barbara Cunningham, Rich Damasko, Joseph Dimartino, Lata
Singh & Elmhurst Hospital Center, Scott Fleischer, Larry Flynt, Steve
Garfinkel, Sal Giarrantano, Josh Greer, Hanft, Bryne, Raboy, Abrams &
Partners, Inc. Sophie Haviland, Ted Hope, Tom O'Donnell, Jr & IBTC
Local 817, Bob & Bill Lincks, David Irving, Jeff Josell, Norman & Michael
Kaufman, Krachman Brothers, Warren LeCruise & The Leo House,
Arnold Mandell, Khated Matar, Payson Meistrich, Shireen Meistrich,
Peter Metsopoulos, Amanda Moore, Jake Myers, Barry Glick, Carol
Lauria, Frank Loprano & The Port Authority of New York & New Jersey,
Thanh Nguyen, Robert F. Nickson, Bill Nisselson, Brendan O'Holleran,
The Ontological Hysteric Theatre, Heta Paarte, Rick Layne, Sarah O'Neil
& The Packer Collegiate Institute, Leonora Cox & St. Paul's Episcopal
Church, Woodside, Queens, Dr Paul Riggs, Anders Bjorck, Linda
Rasmussen & Flemming Alsing at Scandinavian Airlines System (S.A.S.),
Roy Salter, Fern Wakneen, Lowell Williams & The Screen Actors Guild,
Screenplay Systems, Joel Shapiro, Robert M. Smith, Mary Jane Skalski,
Tim Spitzer, Tamarix Capital, Sarah Vogel, Will Flower & Waste
Management of New York, Tom Whelan, Dr Peter Weisel, Irwin Young,
AIM Promotions, Aiwa America, Anheuser-Busch, Anna Sui, Ansell,
Inc. Vista Group, Lucent Technologies, Bary Ridge Funeral Home,
Bollinger Industries, Bunn-O-Matic Corporation, Callard & Bowser-
Suchard, Carhartt, Casio, Inc., The Coca-Cola Company, Premier
Entertainment Services, The Conde Nast Publications, Inc., Fikisha
Cumbo, Dallis Bros. Coffee, The New York Daily News, Dr Martens
AirWair USA, Dow Jones & Company, Triple Dot Communications,
Fargo Electronics, Ferrero USA, F.S. Cameraon, The Gillette Company,
Hamilton College, Heinze, Hunt-Wesson, James River, DDB Needham,

Jetta International, Jussara Lee, Kellogg's Co., Keppler Entertainment, Kitchenaid, Kenneth Cole Productions, Eastman Kodak Company, LFP, Long Life Vitamins, The Mavety Group, New York State Lottery, Nicole Miller, OCS News, Polan Spring/Perrier, PM Promotions, The Pillsbury Company, PO Couture, Princeton Publishing, Quad International, Randell Manufacturing, Rebecca Dandengberg, Samsung Electronics America, Production Resource Center, Swank Publications, Funai Corporation, Times Newsweekly, Up & Company, UPP Entertainment Marketing, US Japan Business News, Utz Quality Foods, The Village Voice, Waste Age Publications, Weber Piano Company, Westpoint Stevens, Xerox Corporation, Zippo Manufacturing Company

Produced on Kodak
Motion Picture Film

International Brotherhood of Teamsters Logo

© New York Daily News, LP
New York Restaurant

Dolby in selected theatres

Filmed with Panavision Cameras & Lenses

This motion picture was made with the cooperation of
the New York City Mayor's Office for Film, Theatre & Broadcasting
and the New Jersey State Film Commission

Filmed entirely on location in New York and New Jersey

The story, all names, characters and incidents portrayed in this motion picture are fictitious. No identification with or any similarities to actual persons, living or dead, or to actual events, is intended or should be inferred.

This motion picture and the soundtrack thereof is protected under the laws of the United States and other countries. Unauthorized duplication, distribution or exhibition may result in civil liability and criminal prosecution.